FEAR

FEAR

A Healthy Emotion If Well Managed

J. Ibeh Agbanyim

FEAR
A Healthy Emotion If Well Managed

iUniverse books may be ordered through booksellers or by contacting:

iUniverse
1663 Liberty Drive
Bloomington, IN 47403
www.iuniverse.com
1-800-Authors (1-800-288-4677)

ISBN: 978-1-4917-1177-4 (sc)
ISBN: 978-1-4917-1178-1 (hc)
ISBN: 978-1-4917-1179-8 (e)

Library of Congress Control Number: 2013918984

Print information available on the last page.

iUniverse rev. date: 02/04/2020

Contents

Endorsements

"Mr. Agbanyim's text on fear is an intriguingly different approach to the construct of fear that may shift the paradigms of thinking on the topic. While I hold strong opinions against viewing fear as a positive emotion, I believe you will find this text worth exploring. It has the potential to contribute new imagination and information to the body of knowledge on fear."

—Lloyd C. Williams, Ph. D., Ph. D., D. Min.,
Organizational Psychologist, CEO, The Institute for
Transformative Thought and Learning, LLC

"Fear is the fundamental instinct of every human being and the greatest fear of all is the fear of death. One of the first steps to living a fulfilled life is to conquer your own fears. Those who don't risk ruining their lives due to FEAR or '*F*alse *E*xpectations *A*ppearing *R*eal.' I applaud Mr. Agbanyim for taking on this tough subject and sharing his in-depth knowledge and inspiring stories. His book allows readers to recognize the 'virus' called fear within various aspects of daily life and also provides a constructive outlook of overcoming it."

—Adil F. Dalal, **CEO, Pinnacle Process Solutions**
International, LLC
Award-winning author of *The 12 Pillars of Project*
Excellence **and** *A Legacy Driven Life*

"Mr. Agbanyim gave us a practical perspective on how to deal with one of the most difficult aspects of life—coping with fear. Fear can be an enemy and a stronghold that prevents us from attaining our individual goals or it can be a catalyst that strengthens us for future challenges. In reality, fear is not always a bad thing. God gave us the capacity to fear so we would not pet a tiger or fall off a tall building. As the author clearly states, fear becomes a negative in our lives when it prevents us from accomplishing personal objectives. The personal examples in this book help us to understand how an intangible like fear can be turned into tangible opportunities in your life. Take advantage of them."

—*Edward D'Avola*, faculty member, University of Phoenix

"This book is deeply insightful and carefully researched on the topic of fear. It addresses the very core of human nature. Life's greatest obstacle is how to overcome inherent fear. Mr. Agbanyim has, through examples and real-life stories, created a ready reckoner and has provided helpful insights to conquer fear. A must-read for every aspiring student, executive, and self-employed person."

—*Raveen Arora*, CEO, India Plaza, and the Dhaba Author of *Laws Relating to Company Auditor* (1975), *New President Ordinances on Trade, Commerce & Industry* (1974), and *Internal Auditing Principles and Practice* (1981)

"For those in the substance abuse counseling profession, this book is a must-read! Although it is not geared specifically toward this population, it can absolutely be applied to patients with addictions. The information provided in this book will be extremely beneficial to therapists when treating their clients. Mr. Agbanyim did a wonderful job explaining fear and makes the topic extremely interesting! Everyone should read this book to learn more about their own fears and why fear is a necessary and productive part of life."

—*Lacey Rojas*, substance abuse counselor

"The ideas shared in this book are written in simple terms which are consistent with the author's first book, *The Power of Engagement: How to Find Balance in Work and Life*. The principles outlined in this book can be applied in every aspect of human endeavors as related to fear. Mr. Agbanyim emphasizes the need to view fear from constructive as opposed to destructive perspectives. I have shared this reading with my sons—as a tool to help motivate them to view fear from a positive scope to improve their skill levels by putting in the extra work needed, whether to earn a starting position on a baseball field or top honors in human anatomy class. This book is a must-read."

—*Isaac Hardy*, manager, Production Control, Turbine Components

"Having just celebrated thirty-five years with my wonderful wife, it was a joy to read the words of Mr. Agbanyim. Married at ages eighteen and nineteen, we faced fears that we had never imagined. With our faith in God and each other, we realized that we had a choice in how we could live our life together. We were fortunate early in our marriage to have the insight that Mr. Agbanyim describes in his book. Life has been so good and will continue that way, because we took control of our fears, not our fears controlling us. Mr.

Agbanyim, thank you for putting together a book that is straightforward and can be read and understood by all ages."

—*Jim Thomas*, Kaiser Aluminum

"If you allow destructive fear to rule your life, you will never experience wonderful opportunities available to you. In twelve years of coaching high school football, I persevered in teaching my athletes how to use constructive fear as a motivator—not only in sports but in their personal lives as well. Mr. Agbanyim has done a great work prescribing how to use destructive fear constructively."

—*Thomas Parson*, high school football coach

"Mr. Agbanyim's work uses the emotion of "fear", which usually can be a life destabilizing trait, and recharacterizes it for constructive purposes. His argument to use fear as a motivator to conquer the things that serve as an impediment to our lives is a unique and most positive approach to self-improvement. His real-world examples helped to easily illustrate his guiding points and his writing is clear and succinct. He writes, "Fear is nothing except a state of mind because it is possible that we see our circumstances the way we are and not the way circumstances are". This line cleanly sums up his thesis in a relatively few amount of words. Many have heard the command to "conquer your fears"; Mr. Agbanyim gives us a model to do just that."

—*Garland Williams, Ph.D., Colonel (ret)*

Preface

After so many years of pretending everything was fine and dandy, it dawned on me that, up until now, fear had been a focal force behind my journey—a journey that linked to so many roads. Some roads were under construction while others were permanently closed. But the truth of the matter remained that fear had been a pivotal ingredient in my journey. Historically, fear shows up anywhere life exists, be it in relationships, workplaces, social settings, or even when we are alone. That is why fear is a *sine qua non* (something absolutely needed) of life. In other words, fear is inevitable. When we start a new job, we fear how other workers will perceive us, how our boss will evaluate us the first time, and if we can be our best selves.

In beginning a relationship, we fear what our partner will think of us and how we can make each other comfortable and fun to be around. In social settings, we fear how our friends will perceive us each time we embark on a new journey. In academic environments, we fear disappointing ourselves in a noticeable manner to our peers and professors.

When I thought about writing my first book, I was terrified and had so many thoughts going through my head, wondering about what-ifs. *Will I ever have enough material* to complete a book? Will my book be worth reading? Will I ever have the right tone to persuade readers to spend some time reading my book(s)? These thoughts were screaming at me day in and day out. Fortunately, I applied positive affirmations to those questions.

In the workplace, I asked myself, *Am I good enough for this position? Can I work hard enough to be considered for promotion and so forth?* But I noticed that, the more I thought about those negative words, the more determined and committed I worked to prove that I was good enough and could succeed.

In my relationships with people, both friends and family, I kept asking myself, *Am I good enough to be considered a friend, brother, student, supervisor, entrepreneur, and so forth?* Again, the more I thought about those words, the more I saw myself challenging those negative voices.

Fast-forwarding to my career and relationship life, I realized that, through all those years of challenging my fears, I was preparing myself for something bigger than life. And as life might have it, many people I encountered over the years have deposited so much into my life. Some were toxic while many were beneficial. But all combined to make me who I am today.

This book came into existence as a result of years of challenges with thoughts that said it could not be done, especially when I decided to embark on my academic journey and met circumstances at work and financial situations that suggested it was impossible. But another thought kept saying, *If you cannot do it for yourself, nobody will do it for you.*

Evidently, silencing those negative thoughts and responding to positive contemplations brought about writing my first book, *The Power of Engagement: How to Find Balance in Work and Life.* This second book is evidence that fearing for the right reasons could propel me to places I never imagined.

With this attitude, I combined practical experiences gathered over the years from customers, clients, professors, family members, and unfamiliar faces—along with time spent reading other people's works and volumes of academic and professional subscriptions—into sharing how fear could work in our favor as opposed to against us. In order to give meaning to this theory of positive fear, I coined productive fears as "constructive fear" while unproductive fears are noted as "destructive fears." So throughout the text, you will notice consistently where I used these words to distinguish how they are operationalized.

In my twenty years of working in logistics, management, entrepreneurship, and so forth, I noticed that people are generally fearful of the unknown and sometimes the known as well. At the same time, people reported that most of the things they fear never happened. This means we create this monster called "failure" in our minds and feed it day after day, week after week, month after month, and year after year until it becomes our way of life. Evidently, if we have admitted our faults about fearing most of the things that never happen, how then do we never make conscious efforts to redirect our thoughts and nourish our ways of thinking and reasoning—enough to allow fear to become a tool for healthy living?

Acknowledgments

To my readers far and near, I thank you for supporting my first book. Your unyielding support encouraged and inspired me to embark on writing the second. I am indebted to your loyalty. To my friends and extended family members, you combined your love to make this work a reality. To my colleagues at work, our everyday clock-in-and-out exercise remains a motivating tool for me. The courage to get up in the morning for the past sixteen years while reporting to work at the same company reminds me of personal commitment to making a positive impact to anybody I meet.

To my photographer and book cover designer, Miss Peace and Miss Uzochwukwu at FotoPlus Concept, I appreciate your dedication and commitment to your work.

To my wife Nnenna Agbanyim and our eight-year-old daughter Comfort, your contributions to my work fortify the family future and demonstrate the efficacy of oneness. Without love investments from loved ones in my life, the ability to produce quality work would be an illusion. So keep up the good work, guys. The closer I get to completion of each project, the more opportunities I encounter. And as long as God drives my life, the journey is always certain and promising for these reasons. "The Lord is my shepherd, I shall not want" (Ps. 23).

To my beloved mother, Madam Comfort, thank you for instilling hope and self-contentment in me. I need those ingredients for my life journey. No amount of money, precious gold, or rubies can buy the qualities you and my late father instilled in me. You have always been instrumental in your advice. You never allowed distance to be a barrier between us for you taught me the true meaning of giving. Even when nothing is left to give, you still give a smile. And I am grateful.

Finally, special thanks to one of my friends and mentors, Professor Phyl Amadi, my unsung hero. I remain loyal to our friendship.

Introduction

Fear has presence. It is a construct that determines our next course of action, especially when seemingly unfamiliar or challenging life events or situations require us to apply critical thinking. But how can we channel our fears to become a source of strength as opposed to a crutch? Before we can respond, we should first understand that fear has presence; therefore, it is real.

Fear can cause a person to slip into emotional paralysis or blur his or her reality.

- A person prematurely quits a job just to avoid being terminated for getting into an argument with his or her supervisor.
- A man murders his pregnant girlfriend, fearing long-term costs of supporting children, the loss of his freedom, the onslaught of parental responsibilities, or a birth that might expose an affair, rape, or sexual abuse of a minor.
- Fearing ridicule, a man avoids public speaking and lives an unfulfilled existence.

- Fearing embarrassment from his mortgage company and friends, a husband abandons his family because he could not provide for them.
- A woman in love with her new boyfriend drowns her own children from her past relationship because her new boyfriend does not like children from another man. She fears her new boyfriend would leave her if she kept her children.
- In fear of being disciplined, a son lies to his mother after he broke a set of glass cups.
- In fear of being invaded, a nation goes to war with its neighboring country.
- Out of fear of losing his or her job, a manager falsifies data to protect his or her position.
- In fear of losing their own lives, a group of New York cops shoots an unarmed civilian fifty times. The unarmed civilian was holding a wallet in his hand while cops misread it for a gun.
- A student drops out of college because he failed one class and his peers teased him so badly. He fears he would find it difficult maintaining good grades to graduate.
- An outstanding math student, who fears not performing well enough in English writing, does not turn in her English paper. In the process, she fails her English writing class.

The list of what fear does to human minds is endless. Clinical psychologist Barbara Markway's article "Getting

Over Stage Fright: Becoming an Effective Public Speaker" shows that fear of public speaking ranks number one while fear of death ranks right behind on what people fear the most in life, which goes to show how much power that fear has in us.

Evidently, fear is powerful. Throughout our young and adult lives, parents, guardians, caregivers, and so forth, tell us that fear is negative and carries the presence of disruption. So we assume that nothing constructive comes out of fear. Little do we know that fear can be a healthy emotion for success.

The focus of this book will draw from life events supported by evidence-based studies that depict fear as constructive and healthy because we already know what damages unhealthy fear can cause to life. Therefore, emphasis will focus on how fear operates as relating to human relationships—whether in social settings or workplaces—and how healthy fear has motivated scientists and nonscientists alike to create positive changes that influence the world.

Chapter 1

Fear: A Figment of Our Imagination?

The first process to living a life full of hope, success, faith, and spiritual growth is to admit that fear is real—be it fear of failure in a relationship, workplace, or academic pursuits or facing our biggest breakthrough in a relationship, promotion in the workplace, or winning the Best Researcher of the Year Award. Our success in life is birthed from fear of failing—be it fear of living alone, becoming homeless, ending up an object of mockery, and so forth. When we understand that, instead of running away from the very thing that handicaps our success, we learn to face it constructively by actually defining what makes us fear that thing, why we cannot face it, and how to face it. Overcoming our internal prison walls is easy. In other words, if we can allow our fears to push us into life breakthroughs, we can live a life of fulfillment. Therefore, we should embrace fear with confidence and boldness because, as corporate bodies, we cannot conquer what we cannot confront. And the only way to conquer our fears is to shift our thought process in the direction of learning and investigating the unknown I call ignorance, a quest to know.

Dr. Stuart Firestein, a neuroscientist and chairman of the Department of Biology at Columbia University, who has published over one hundred papers in scientific and scholarly journals, profoundly noted that knowledge is a big subject, but ignorance is a larger one. Therefore, the ability to position ourselves to learn what we don't know will minimize, if not eliminate, fear of avoiding our life challenges, especially learning from a position of ignorance for a good cause. We perceived from childhood that fear is real and has negative connotations, but we lack the understanding of how fear can equip us into achieving greatness. Evidently, fear has presence, one that could distort self-awareness, sense of purposefulness, and social norms. On the other hand, the understanding of how fear can compel a person to see beyond the obvious and ordinary is what this book is all about.

This book is not a substitute to counseling or legal advice. It serves as additional information that can help us better understand the efficacy of fear and the ways we can use it to achieve positive results. This book does not advise readers to undermine emergency situations that life occasionally offers. Rather, we should handle emergency situations with clarity and a sense of urgency by calling the appropriate individuals or authorities for assistance. Emergency situations occur regularly, but responding to them requires clarity and focus.

The incidences of shootings at US schools (Newtown, Virginia Tech, and Columbine), shopping malls (Clackamas Mall, Oregon), and movie theaters (Aurora) reveal it is appropriate to be concerned in certain places where the shootings might happen. Recently, a man discussed his experience at a movie theater on Christmas Day. While the movie was playing, the lights were dimmed, and the audio was loud. A man of average height sitting three rows in front of him got up and leaned against a handrail on the walk path inside the movie theater. A few minutes later, he walked up all the way to the last row and sat, resting his legs in front of his seat. His erratic behavior raised suspicion and fear, especially after reading and watching the Aurora movie theater shooting in the news.

Based on this illustration, what would you do if you were in that movie theater? Evidently, one or two things will happen. You either move to a different row (away from the erratic man) or leave the movie theater entirely out of fear. This illustration demonstrates how powerful fear can be to our consciousness, and while this is not the focus of this book, it is worth mentioning because fear is real.

In this chapter, we examine how fear operates in the minds of people in workplaces and relationships. We will introduce two terms, destructive and constructive fear, our operational words to distinguish between good and bad fear. In other words, good fear is when the outcome is mutual and progressive. For example, during economic downturns, some employers reduced employee workweeks to four days on a ten-hour shift, as opposed to five days on an eight-hour shift.

This departmental restructuring saves both companies and employees some operational cost. The price of running production for an extra day, lighting bills, building maintenance, and miscellaneous risks associated with operating a business could be avoided by working longer hours during a shorter workweek. Employees, on the other hand, would enjoy three days of rest per week, prevent wear and tear of their cars, and spend time with their loved ones. Employers take this approach (four-day workweeks) to avoid downsizing, fearing that not acting will save workers' jobs.

Conversely, bad fear is simply when the result creates a retrogressive effect. For example, a manager fears losing his or her job. Instead of finding an effective way to increase productivity through collaboration, he or she instead increases disciplinary action, intending to terminate employees and whereby pleasing his or her boss and crushing employee morale.

Presence of Fear in the Workplace

In the workplace, managers and employees ought to acknowledge that destructive fear impairs learning, improvement, and relationships. In other words, a manager who uses destructive fear tactics to manage employees is simply creating an environment that will affect employees' ability to effectively perform their job tasks.

When destructive fear cripples the ability to learn, improvement in the workplace becomes an illusion. The employer-employee relationship is also affected when the work environment is unfriendly. That is, when managers are more interested in productivity and less concerned about employees' welfare, they become more critical of each other. Therefore, managing employees from a position of destructive fear tactics can essentially backfire.

For example, some of the subtle ways of using fear tactics in managing employees are micromanagement and microaggressive behaviors. Micromanagement focuses on managers who oversee workers too closely and spend an excessive amount of time supervising a specific job task by instructing employees precisely what to do and how to do it. Such closeness is considered compulsive monitoring.

John, a middle-aged employee, worked customer service at a local hotel in town for three years. Tim, his new supervisor, was transferred from the East Coast to replace a retiring service supervisor with thirty-two years of experience. Tim had never worked or lived on the West Coast before. He was a bit tense, anxious, and nervous about this shift in culture. Instead of sharing his genuine fear with his employee John and getting to know his employee, he decided to pretend that everything was fine.

On one occasion, while John was greeting a guest who walked to the front counter for a room inquiry, Tim stood behind John, whispering to him how he should greet a guest. John accepted his advice and pleasantly asked the guest how he could help. Tim jumped in again and asked John to smile more pleasantly. John accepted and did what Tim suggested.

As the guest was inquiring for room rates, Tim whispered to John, "Show the guest the least expensive rooms first and then the most expensive next."

John could not concentrate because Tim kept interrupting. As John was pointing out different rooms and bed sizes, Tim whispered to John to ask the guest how many days he was staying. After completing the transaction with the guest, John handed the guest keys to his room and motioned directions to the elevator. Immediately, Tim asked John if he could have offered the guest a bigger room for convenience and at a higher rate. John felt unappreciated and underestimated. Tim never praised John for his pleasantness to the guest. Instead, he expected more out of John.

If you were John, how would you feel? If we really think about John and Tim's situation, we find ourselves in an unfamiliar circumstance on a daily basis. We tend to pretend and respond defensively. Therefore, nobody is immune to Tim and John's experiences; the approach method makes a world of difference, especially the way Tim handled his fear, which was destructive and unproductive.

Constructive Fear Approach

Oftentimes, individuals in the workplace fear one issue or another—for example, low productivity, poor performance, safety, job loss, and so forth. But what makes such fear destructive is when we focus too much on negative results. Now let's flip the same issues to be constructive. When productivity is low, instead of fearing losing one's job, we fear for the company closing down and affecting more than just the employees or management. The families of employees and managers are equally impacted. Thinking of the bigger impact would drive away negative fear and encourage both employer and employees to find a corporate solution rather than seek out an individual solution. Because of a fear that the entire organization will go out of business, everybody benefits from finding a way to rescue the company from collapsing. This is an example of constructive fear, solving individual problems as corporate rather than individual problems. In other words, we have the mind-set of "what affects one affects all." Therefore, think globally and act locally. Fear constructively by thinking how to turn your fears into an opportunity.

The way we handle fear determines the outcome. Fear can encourage a manager to promote, demote, or fire an employee. If a manager promotes an employee, that means the employee's economic, social, and relationship status and organizational growth will improve.

1. The employee will have a sense of meaningfulness.
2. The employee will gain more confidence.
3. Personal and family quality of life will increase as a result of one single act from a manager.

On the other hand, firing a worker affects employee morale, self-worth, confidence, economic status, and relationships. Unless an employee violates company policy and proper disciplinary action is followed, then the company does not commit any fault.

Based on this brief analysis, if you are a manager, which side of the fence would you prefer: to discharge employees out of fear or to retain employees out of fear? Whatever answer you choose, ask yourself, *Am I acting out of constructive or destructive fear? Am I acting to protect my selfish interest, or is it based on selfless motives?* When we base our judgment on selfless motives, we tend to make sound decisions and ignore self-biases and prejudices. Self-biases often are rooted in our life experiences, especially when such encounters are negative and fill us with regret.

For example, some people who grew up poor in terms of economic deprivations tend to carry that mentality along, and as a result of their experiences, they find it difficult to help another person financially, fearing they may bankrupt themselves if they help others. Such thoughts bring about poverty mentality, one that subjects people to focus on what they do not have as opposed to concentrating on what they do have.

The next chapter discusses what poverty mentality really means and how behaviors are directly related to people's background and experiences. As we read chapter 2, ask, *How do our experiences contribute to our actions in a particular situation? Are we allowing our family backgrounds and financial struggles to dictate our decisions and interactions with others?*

Hopefully, chapter 2 will shed some light on how to overcome poverty mentality.

Chapter 2

Poverty Mentality

The poverty mentality attitude of thinking remains a human struggle because it robs us of the opportunity of focusing on what we have as opposed to what we do not. This mentality causes us to hold on to the familiar and never let go even when it is uncomfortable and destructive to our future. Let's use an illustration to describe what poverty mentality really means. Zig Ziglar pointed out that, by focusing on what is missing in our lives rather than focusing on what is there, this can lead to further poverty.

Tim Cestnick, author of *101 Tax Secrets for Canadians*, narrated his experience during his estate planning conference that took place on a cruise ship in the Caribbean. On the third day of the cruise, the ship stopped by St. Thomas. While Tim and his family were eating lunch, Tim noticed about twenty parrots of different sizes and colors sitting on their perches. Not one was in a cage, which made it awkward and interesting why they didn't just fly away.

Out of curiosity, Tim asked the parrot keeper, "Why do none of these parrots want to fly away?"

The parrot keeper answered, "I trained them all to think that their perches are where they will be safe and secure. Once they believe this, they tightly wrap their claws around the perch, and they don't want to let go. They keep themselves confined. It's almost as though they have forgotten how to fly, although I know they could if they tried."

This anecdote applies to us. We hold on to our past experiences to the point that we never want to change, and when we fail to adapt, we cling onto our limited dogmas. For example, we may eat only once a day because food and money were scarce during adolescence. But now that we have made it better than ever, we still hold on to the past that could rob us of our future. When we hold on to what we have without thinking about other possibilities of expanding, we remain stagnant and stingy. It is the "glass half-full versus glass half-empty" syndrome. As long as we think our glass is half-empty, we will always be struggling, but if we see life as a glass half-full, we start to shift our thinking in a positive direction. Shifting our thoughts to be hopeful and grateful paves the way for more opportunities to come to us. Seeing our past as a promise rather than a curse would encourage us to turn our ashes into beautiful, our disgrace into grace, and our lamentation into laughter. All these things can occur if we liberate ourselves from the grip of poverty mentality, which is nothing but a distorted perception.

Jennifer Kunst, PhD, a clinical psychologist and psychoanalyst, noted in her recent 2012 article in *Psychology Today* that perspective is everything. When we concentrate our future so much on our past, we tend to repeat what we have always known. For example, consider a student who failed a second-grade math class and tried again in fourth grade and failed. The most dangerous thing to do is to assume that he or she is bad at math. To perceive failure in math establishes an evidence of math phobia. As a result, we fail to learn math. Such action indicates poverty mentality—that is, focusing on what we don't have rather than focusing on what we do have. A student who wants to overcome the fear of failing math is to focus on thirty-nine other courses he or she performs exceptionally well in (based on undergrad program).

Past experiences are simply that. If retrieving from the past does not improve the present, then there is no need to entertain such thoughts. In other words, when you remember what happened to you when you were nine years old, for example, and become angry, bitter, resentful, aloof, withdrawn, and revengeful, then you basically harm yourself even more. Such toxic emotions cripple human potentials and rob us from living a life full of promise.

Evidently, we cannot change the past, but we can definitely choose the course of action in remodeling our present and future. Therefore, to not fear ever living a life of lack, emptiness, and spiritual paralyses would essentially force us to do the opposite of what could land us in awkward positions.

An elderly, wealthy (spiritually and financially) man once told me, "If you want to be successful in whatever you do, do the opposite of what poor people do."

In this context, poverty is not limited to financial lack in any sense, but it extends to our pattern of thinking (poverty mentality). By implication, the worse poverty mentality pattern is the inability to think creatively, critically, and constructively. When our thinking lacks any of these constructs (creative, critical, and constructive), it sets a stage for thought breakdown.

Let's use the above example of a student who struggles in math. Failing math class is not the problem. Instead, idolizing and entertaining such thoughts is more damaging than failing itself. Instead of fearing math from a perspective of failing it again, fear math from a viewpoint of doing whatever it takes not to fail math. When we allow our thought pattern to fear math so much so that we stay away from it, we remain a slave to math. But when we fear it so much that we master math, we triumph. In this scenario, one is destructive fear (fear of failing math), and the other is constructive fear (fear to a point of mastering math).

One approach to solving the problem of destructively fearing math is thinking about our thinking. In psychology, it is called metacognition.

Metacognition

A study shows that about twelve thousand to sixty thousand thoughts flow through our brain on a daily basis. Evidently, several thoughts are to be processed in a day.

Connecting our thoughts with this chapter about poverty mentality allows us to ask thought-provoking questions. *What do we think about? Could it be possible that our thinking produces results when applied (both bad and good thoughts)?* That is a resounding yes. We are what we think about. So if we think about failure, we fail. If we think about success, we succeed. It is that simple. But it is easier said than done because it requires self-discipline and self-efficacy (knowing thyself). It is important that we ask ourselves, *Who are we?* When we think about that, we also engage in metacognition, a process of thinking about our thinking.

Now let's think about our fears right at this moment. Are we thinking about them in terms of obstacles or opportunities? Are we thinking about how they can transform or deform us? Are we thinking about how fear has led great minds to invent ideas that changed our lives forever (for example, Thomas Edison; PhD; Dr. Albert Bandura; Justice Sonia Sotomayor; Dr. Martin Luther King Jr.; and so forth)? Or are we thinking about how fear has led challenged minds to destroy lives in a matter of seconds?

As people, we go through these mental exercises every day, and we probably practice self-efficacy more than we give ourselves credit for. When we think about what we are thinking, we allow ourselves to reexamine our thoughts (metacognition/thinking about our thinking). Therefore, challenge yourself today by examining your fears from constructive perspectives. For example, we say to ourselves, "I fear I will starve to death if I don't get a job" or "I will lose my spouse if I don't keep my house at peace." Those are raw emotions because they decide the next course of action.

In 2006, a team of researchers (Trevor Moores, Jerry Cha-Jan Chang, and Deborah Smith) made a profound statement that thinking about our thoughts allows us to know how well we are performing and how we are likely to be accurate or wrong in our judgment. Based on this information, we can argue that we are aware of how our thoughts will turn out when they are acted out. This means, when we endow ourselves with destructive fears, the result will likely reflect our fears. And if we think of fear in a sense of an opportunity to prove ourselves, then we drive away poverty mentality.

Therefore, let us rethink our thoughts. This exercise changes behavior and our actions. So, guide your thoughts, reexamine them, test your assumptions, be open-minded about the result of your thoughts, and be willing to change when necessary. Through mental exercises, we come to believe in ourselves and fear's potency.

The next chapter focuses on why we should believe in fear. In other words, fear—be it destructive or constructive—drives our daily activities. It is an indisputable presence in whatever we do. Therefore, we should accept that fear is a part of human existence and we should believe it in order to carefully navigate and discern between good and bad fear.

Chapter 3

Believe in Fear

Believe in fear's potency. It is impossible to live a fear-free life. But we can decide what type of fear—constructive or destructive—to operate on. Therefore, the type of fear we believe in determines our level of approach. Let's use a true story to illustrate this point of believing in fear's potency.

Kim Farino, a nutritionist and a certified personal trainer who graduated from Dowling College in New York, wrote a memoir, *Thank God for Another Day: The Miracle Breakthrough*, in which she shared her darkest secrets when she battled with drugs and alcohol. This all stemmed from her inability to express herself because her parents always told her to be grateful for what she had and never complain about anything. Growing up, she learned not to express herself about anything other than gratefulness.

Tragically, at the age of seven, her neighbor, one her parents loved, exposed Kim to inappropriate touching and fondling. She kept it secret for fear of being accused of complaining. At the age of sixteen, the same neighbor molested her.

They were a young married couple, Barbie and Tom, who moved into the neighborhood. The young wife quickly got comfortable with Kim's mother because Barbie was a dance instructor and Kim loved dancing. Kim's mother trusted Barbie to give little Kim dance lessons after school. Unbeknownst to Kim's mother, Tom would take advantage of her trust by molesting sixteen-year-old Kim.

Fast-forward to Kim's adult life: her drug and alcohol abuse got so bad that, even when she was married and had a child, she still couldn't stop. Her addictions were so bad that she was in and out of rehab, seeking help. Her breakthrough happened on her last day at a detox center when her doctor and nurse were preparing her discharge papers. The doctor asked what her next plan was. Kim was more interested in washing her hair and getting good sleep in her own bed. Her doctor and nurse looked at her with confusion on their faces.

Finally, the doctor told Kim, "Do you understand how serious this is? This is life or death for you. You will not make it back if you don't take this disease seriously. It will kill you. Please take this list of support groups and therapists that can help you."

As Kim was getting ready to leave the detox center, she confided in her nurse that she felt safer in the detox center.

But her nurse responded, "Honey, that's called fear. That's a good feeling because that fear will keep you from picking up that first drink. Keep that fear close to your heart, and remember that God has so much better plans for you."

Kim has been sober since 2005. The moral of her story is that she experienced both destructive and constructive fear. In the midst of it all, she made a conscious decision to stick with constructive fear, which has kept her sober for this many years. Her decision to quit drugs and alcohol saved her marriage. Evidently, that fear, when constructively applied, could have a ripple effect. In other words, it has a positive influence in other areas of our lives. In this case, personal and marital relationships were restored. How can we apply constructive fear in our own relationships?

Believe in Constructive Fear When in a Relationship

Wendy Walsh, PhD, author of *The 30-Day Love Detox*, noted that divorce teaches us how to divorce, and that's it. In other words, if you already know how to get divorced, the more likely you will see it as an option. To support Dr. Walsh's claim, Mara Opperman, a relationship expert, noted a study that shows that an estimated 67 to 80 percent of second marriages end in divorce while third marriages dwindle at an even higher rate. This is an astounding claim because, if people knew the survival rate of their second or third marriages was slim to none, chances are, they would rather work on their first. In this case, with the exception of marital abuse (verbal, emotional, physical, and so forth), married couples are better off working on their first marriage rather than experiencing marriage marathon (going from one marriage to another).

How does this apply to the fear factor? Except in a case of marital abuse, destructive fear drives most marriages into divorce. In other words, people fear that, if they stay in their troubled unions, they will never be happy again. As a result of their untested assumption, they prefer divorce. On the contrary, couples who know that divorcing their spouses would increase their chances of multiple divorces will stay to make their marriage work. Therefore, believing in constructive fear is critical in a relationship because it changes the course of action. First, information transforms a person; lack of it deforms someone.

Now that we know that not all fears are destructive, we can then reexamine our fears, especially in terms of marriage or in a relationship. Oftentimes (if not all of the time), the very thing that separates couples is the very quality that brought them together in the first place. Generally, when people get married, they expect to improve their quality of life. We never plan to get a divorce when we go into a relationship. After the expectations are hampered, divorce then becomes an option. Therefore, if couples would focus on improving quality of life by constructively fearing not to divorce each other, such marriages would survive the test of time. The fear alone of not getting a divorce would encourage couples to constructively work on their marriages.

Kim was already using drugs and drinking heavily when she married Anthony. Interestingly, her husband was a cool-headed and completely responsible man, but as love would have it, he fell in love with Kim even after knowing about her drug problems. After their honeymoon, she feared losing her husband from her drug use. That same fear of losing her husband kept her going back to rehab to stay sober. In the end, she applied constructive fear and restored her marriage.

Evidently, our worst enemy is ourselves. When we fail to turn off those negative voices screaming inside of us, telling us we are insecure and incompetent, we eventually start to believe those destructive voices. Can we apply Kim's theory for a minute? She wrote her memoir to shut down those little demons telling her she could never be free from drugs and drinking, remain happily married, or have a normal life. Instead, she told that inner voice, *The darkness in my life changes to radiant light when I realize that being truthful and honest with myself and others will bring me the serenity, peace, and freedom I search and crave for on a daily basis.*

If you believe in constructive fear, you will have the right to self. In other words, in the journey for success, only one person—self—is in charge. So, believe in self and the potency of constructive fear. When you believe in constructive fear, you believe in the principle of God that states, "The fear of the Lord is the beginning of wisdom" (Prov. 9:10a; Ps. 111:10a).

By implication, not all fears are evil or negative. Constructive fear leads to transformational renewal of thoughts. And when we are transformed in our way of thinking, we tend to see challenges from different perspectives, ones that allow us to look again, question, and test our initial views. Kim's memoir is evidence that constructive fear liberates a captive from his or her dogmas. If she would have failed to reexamine her fears, she would have repeated her known behavior, which was to drink and drug away her life. Instead, she rose above her familiar pattern of thinking and risked thinking outside of the box. She allowed herself to relive her childhood pains when she went into a three-day healing program, one her therapist conducted, where her therapist gave her permission to act out her past childhood memories with a complete stranger. Through that exercise, she gave herself permission to accept the little child inside of her, the one who had been trying to express herself all these years. After the third day of therapy, she began to feel free and peaceful inside of her, evidence of total forgiveness of herself and freedom to a new beginning.

In this context, constructive fear is a believable exercise. Constructive fear is, in essence, an exercise. Why so? Remind yourself, when the urge of drinking or drugging yourself comes, find other things you love doing (besides drinking and drugging) and engage your mind in those things. If possible, start doing those things as soon as you can get to them. When you do that, you drive away destructive fear and activate healthy fear of doing nourishing habits.

In Kim's situation, she revisited the feeling she had when she first celebrated the little girl inside of her without locking up the little girl's unconsciousness. Focus on that feeling and memory of the best thing that ever happened to you. When you do that, rather than running away from fear completely, you run to fear constructively by remembering happy moments.

The next chapter discusses what it means to fear failure. Fear of failure can elevate you to a new height or plunge you to oblivion. Let us journey together in an attempt to explore fear using true life stories to support why fear of failure could evidently motivate one to live a life of difference in the face of challenges.

Chapter 4

Constructive Fear of Failure

Is it a bad thing to fear failure? This is an honest question to ask. History has it that some fundamental things can never be known with certainty. That is why nothing is definite.

- If life is definite, why is a baby born without arms or legs without any medical explanation or warning?
- Two patients will visit the same doctor for an identical sickness. The doctor will prescribe the same medications to both, yet one will recover with ease while the other will prolong his illness.
- Two brothers are raised in the same home with the same parents. One goes his way to higher learning; the other heads to prison for multiple criminal charges.
- Two sisters attend the same school and live in the same home. One excels in mathematics; the other struggles.

We should understand that life is what it is. The difference is the attitude with which we view it. Some view life pessimistically; others perceive life with optimism. Evidently, fear of failure is the beginning of success. It is the beginning of success that, if we acknowledge that fear is natural, it cannot be dismissed or treated as nonexistence. Therefore, we should entertain fear with hopefulness and exuberance.

In this chapter, we read about a young man named Nick Vujicic who was born without arms or legs. Yet his life story has impacted millions around the globe. It is evidence of the presence of constructive fear of failure. In other words, if we constructively fear failure, we are likely to do something that would counteract the very thing we fear. In the case of Nick Vujicic, the fear of living life permanently depending on parents and friends compelled him to be constructive in order to be independent, using all other potentials God had blessed him with to secure his freedom or independence.

As we read this chapter, think about how we can lift ourselves up from fear of failure through applying positive psychology in areas beyond human comprehension. For example, in the case of Nick Vujicic, evidence (born with no arms and no legs) suggests he would not be able to take care of himself, let alone find a soul mate or permanent friend. But his fear of becoming what the obvious suggested motivated him to challenge the palpable. Therefore, in an attempt to prove that his constructive fear approach to life generates confidence, focus, optimism, and success in the face of challenges, this is why this chapter uses Nick's adequacies rather than inadequacies to demonstrate how constructive fear of failure is evidently a force for fulfillment.

The Story of Nick Vujicic

Without exhausting readers with Nick's story, we would gain basic knowledge about him and build a case around his successes to justify why constructive fear of failure is critical. Nick Vujicic was born without arms or legs to Pastor Boris and Nurse Dushka Vujicic in Melbourne, Australia. He had early childhood challenges in school due to his disabilities, which led him to suffer from low self-esteem, depression, and loneliness. His loving parents and friends were his bedrock, but his encouragement came from his faith in God. His faith and focus in life sustained him to obtain double bachelor's degrees in accounting and financial planning from Griffith University in Logan, Australia. His career took off at the age of nineteen when he started impacting people with his life experiences. As of 2008, he had traveled to about fourteen countries and presented to over two million people.

This statistical evidence shows that:

1. Our ability to remove mental limitations in life is more powerful than the atomic bomb. Mental limitations are those negative thoughts that paralyze us. In Nick's case, evidence shows that, if he would have dwelled in the lonely space of self-pity, chances are, he would have missed his calling to use his disabilities to demonstrate the awesomeness of God. In this context, he has touched over two million people as a result of a shift in his thinking. All of those people would have never been impacted had he lived a life of self-pity.

2. His ability to imagine something bigger than himself propelled him to the very thing he admired. As of 2013, Nick is married to his beautiful wife, and they have a beautiful child together. During interviews, he mentioned he would never have thought anybody would love him to the point of marrying him, but his fear of living a life of loneliness forced him to act on the very fear that was meant to paralyze him.

3. His courage to speak on his disability made his case public and allowed the world to see him for who he is, a kindhearted, intelligent, loving, and humble man. In the process of making his case public, circumstance presented a beautiful lady, whom he married.

Note that Nick did not wrap himself inside his house waiting for a miracle to happen; rather, he exposed his fear to the world, and the world came to his rescue by offering him those things that he called upon: happiness, peacefulness, acceptance, sense of belonging, and fulfillment. Notice that all of the qualities that made Nick successful were intangible—hopefulness, imagination, determination, commitment, discipline, and steadfastness.

The Relevance of the Story

Every one of us has Nick's disability—the sense of rejection, abandonment, aloofness, insecurity, incompetence, blame, and so forth—inside of us. On the other hand, we also have Nick's unlimited imagination, immeasurable sense of kindness, humility, caring, focus, and so forth. Whose voice are we hearing? Is it the voice of inadequacy or abundance? You can only answer this question if you understand the unlimited access you have inside of you. Nick tapped into this unlimited access when he decided to apply constructive fear that suggested, *If I don't do it for myself, nobody will. If I can make it through college, why can't I make it in life? If I can control my own happiness, why can't I live a life of abundance?* Each and every one of us has been in a position where we feel life has forsaken us, the same feeling Nick had. Yet most of us were born with two arms and two legs. If we compare our lives with Nick's, we stand a better chance of living a more meaningful life based on the natural norms, yet we are not living a life that supports natural norms. Natural norms or common sense suggest that a person who has all body parts has a better chance of surviving than a person who doesn't. In this instance, who is disabled, Nick or you?

Making a Difference

Nick changed his story when he adapted his thinking patterns. Early in this chapter, I mentioned how Nick thought he would never meet anybody who would love him for him. But as he challenged his own thoughts through traveling to all corners of the world and witnessing many situations, he realized that people needed him despite his disability. He is actually an inspiration to millions of people. In that process, opportunity presented itself as Nick positioned himself to possibilities. In this instance, Nick rewrote his own history, one that was meant to be remembered as a man with no arms and no legs who lived without a future, family, children, or happiness. Instead, he wants to be remembered as a man who made a difference in the lives of millions of people. He's a father, husband, motivational speaker, and a happy, peaceful man.

Can you challenge your life by saying, "If Nick can live a life of fulfillment, I can too"? The only force that can make this affirmation a reality is constructive fear. If you can say, "I am tired of living a life of mediocre, and I want a change," when you do this, you will position yourself to look again and do things differently. Until we rethink and take different courses of action, we can never liberate ourselves from the bondage we find ourselves in. Albert Einstein noted, "The significance of issues we face cannot be resolved at the same level of thinking we were at when we created them," suggesting that, if we want a change, we must take a different approach to our issues. Nick makes a significant impact in the world by shifting his thinking and imagination from destructive to constructive fear. If we do what Nick is doing, chances are, we would remove those prison walls that keep us from living life to the fullest.

Evidently, we build those prison walls (destructive fear of failure) in our minds and actually idolize those walls as our reality. Destructive fear of failure comprises so many components—for example, fear of exposing our weaknesses in the workplace, relationships, or social settings. But how certain are we about what people may say or do to us? Chances are, people are so busy grappling with their own issues that they have less time to gossip about you. But even if they did gossip about you—so what? Almost seven billion people are on earth, and you are worried about a handful of people who barely know your entire story. Life is bigger than gossip and destructive fear because gossip exists in the absence of goals and dreams. Therefore, we should not spend too much time worried about a few people who do not like us. Instead, concentrate on the positive side of life.

In the case of Nick, he refused to allow gossip and public ridicule to distract him from his goals. If we allow ourselves to entertain gossip, we are evidently writing our checks over to those who gossip against us and empowering them to take charge of our future. Is that really what you want, to mortgage your future to a group of gossipmongers with less enthusiasm in discovering their own courses of life? Don't give away your power to the voice of doom. When the voice of doom is getting too loud, raise your standard by focusing on your dreams—that is, by challenging yourself to conquer what confronts you.

If you fail to confront what confronts you, you will find yourself in a lonely state of mind called defeat. In that mind-set, it can be difficult to triumph or sing when your world is closing up on you. Live a life of transformation, not one of deformation.

The next chapter poses a thought-provoking question. If we did what we felt was transformational and life still offered us unending challenges, could we sing a song when we were in the valley of tears? This question is not that easy to answer because it depends on so many variables. The nature and magnitude of challenges matters.

This next chapter will explore different scenarios, including sharing a true story of Horatio Spafford, a young lawyer who was also a successful real estate dealer. Tragedy struck in the Great Chicago Fire and devastated the entire city. He lost almost all of his assets. As if that were not enough, he experienced another terrible tragedy that could have brought a brave man to his knees.

This chapter is intended to challenge our imagination and faith in times of trouble. As you read this chapter, ask yourself, *Can I be optimistic and hopeful in the midst of life-devastating circumstances?* Reflect on life events that once pushed you to the wall, and think about how you could have responded differently. In other words, as you read this chapter, put yourself in the characters' positions to empathize, sympathize, or show no apathy. Whatever feeling you experienced, write it down as soon as you felt it. This exercise will capture your raw feeling.

Ask yourself, *Am I seeing this challenge for what it is, or am I inflating the situation?* Being present with your feelings will help you deal with the circumstances more distinctly without cluttered emotions. Hopefully, this chapter will shed different lights on how to approach life struggles.

Chapter 5

Can You Sing a Song When You
Are in the Valley of Tears?

Every one of us has, in one event or another, encountered situations that tested our faith. Certain life situations seem unbearably difficult to survive, especially when you have given it all. People who went through a horrible divorce, for example, can attest to this experience, especially when children were involved and custody was inevitably part of the process. A spouse felt uncontrollable dread when divorce proceedings were fast approaching, a feeling that brought destructive fear and anger at the same time. There's the fear of uncertainty and the fear of wonderment. *If I divorce him or her, will anybody ever love me again? What would our children think about me? What kind of person am I? Will I ever be happy again?* The list is endless. The pains and fear become inescapable prison walls.

In this state of mind, peace of mind seems unattainable, nights seem never ending, and days crawl at a snail's pace. While everybody around you seems to be enjoying life, your own seems to be ending. Hell becomes real on earth; heaven becomes a utopia. Your spouse, once a source of joy, is now your worst nightmare.

In the midst of these heartaches and wonderment, can you sing a song of praise and still be optimistic? It takes skills and discipline to know what to do under this vulnerable position. It takes mental discipline to remember, "Yea, though I walk through the valley of the shadow of death, I fear no evil; for you are with me" (Ps. 23:4). Only when you know the source of your strength can you say, "It is well with my soul." In substance, you are saying, even though you know calamity has befallen you, you know who holds tomorrow; therefore, destructive fear will not hold you hostage. This affirmation is practical because history has it that brave people have conquered their fears through affirmation and positive actions. For example, consider Martin Luther King Jr., Nelson Mandela, Nick Vujicic (chapter 4), Andrea Bocelli, Horatio Spafford, and so forth.

Horatio Spafford proved to the world that the human mind could activate memorized emotions (one a person recalls when experiencing a similar situation) in times of difficulties and pains. In the case of Horatio Spafford, he was able to survive the loss of his real estate in the Great Chicago Fire in 1871. Surviving the fire and another great tragedy led him to produce one of the most widely sang hymns in the world, "It Is Well with My Soul."

When Horatio Spafford composed the hymn in 1873, he did not write it when the sky was blue and the house was full of smiley and happy faces. Rather, he wrote it when his world caved in on him, one of the darkest days of his time. Take a moment, and recollect when you had your worst tragedy of all time. Horatio Spafford, in that mental state, birthed "It Is Well with My Soul," a song that has brought consolation and comfort to many people who are experiencing pains and grief. Although it was composed out of grief, it gives hope to the hopeless and laughter to the lamented.

In 1871, Horatio Spafford was a successful lawyer who owned several real estate assets. He was also a great husband to Anna and father to their four daughters, a family setting anybody would wish to have. As fate would have it, in October of that same year, a fire in Chicago reduced the city to ashes, along with Horatio Spafford's properties. This tragedy really affected Horatio Spafford financially and emotionally. He tried staying happy and positive to his family without letting the fire take away his peace and joy. But in light of such devastating events, life challenges never stops.

In 1873, two years after the disaster, the family decided to take a vacation cruise ship called *Ville du Havre* to Europe with friends, a way of rejuvenating their devastating lives from the fire. Incidentally, at the last minute, a business deal, one he needed to finalize before joining his family on vacation, delayed Horatio Spafford. He decided for his wife and four daughters to go ahead without him. He would join them later. Considering what had happened to the family's real estate business two years prior, it was wise for him to stay back and finalize the business deal before joining them.

On November 21, 1873, the British iron sailing ship *Lochearn* rammed the luxurious steamer, and within twelve minutes of the impact, the *Ville du Havre* sank in the middle of the Atlantic Ocean. Tragically, none of Horatio's daughters survived. Only his wife was saved, and she sailed by a cargo vessel to Cardiff, Wales, nine days later.

Anna cabled her husband Horatio with a few words: "saved alone. What shall I do . . .?" It's a question nobody would ever want to read from his or her loved one. Could you imagine how shocking and emotionally paralyzed Horatio was? This man's life was shattered from the Great Chicago Fire, and now he had another tragedy of losing his four precious daughters. Life events could be a mystery.

After receiving the devastating cable (message) from his wife Anna, he immediately left Chicago to bring his wife home. While sailing on the Atlantic Ocean, the captain of his ship called Horatio to his cabin to inform him that they were passing over the spot where his four daughters had perished, three miles deep in the waters. Horatio consoled himself by pretending that his four daughters were not in that watery grave. Rather, "they are safe, folded, the dear lambs." While in deep pain, he wrote "It Is Well with My Soul."

In our night of tears, how many can sing a song like Horatio did? He essentially understood that, in the face of sorrow and agony, if we can ever remember what God has ever done for us, we could still show gratitude. In his case, although his four precious daughters died in the process but his wife survived, this means there is hope in the face of hopelessness. By implication, he feared that, although life would never be the same, he should show gratitude to God for saving his wife from the grip of death. What can we learn from Horatio's optimistic attitude in the face of woes?

Lessons to Be Learned in the Face of Adversity

Debbie Ford, an internationally recognized expert in the field of personal transformation and a pioneer in emotional and spiritual education, said, "Pain causes opening if we allow it to." In other words, if we can allow our painful situation to teach us what it is to be a human being, then we can come out of it better than we were because pain teaches us how to be humble and reach to a higher power if we allow it to.

Dr. Peter Senge, professor at Massachusetts Institute of Technology and founding chair of the Society for Organizational Learning, said, "If there is a kind of way to have a moment of pause and we all became aware of something, I will say to wake up." Situations of life have a way of waking us up. In Horatio's tragedy, he composed the most widely sang hymn when life situations drove him to compose a masterpiece, as "it is well with my soul."

Dr. Joe Dispenza, who completed his postgraduate training and education on neurology, neuroscience, brain function, and chemistry, said, "Human beliefs are connected to our feelings." Therefore, in times of adversity, our beliefs activate our feelings. As a result, we respond to situations based on our recorded beliefs and feelings. In essence, pay attention to your beliefs and feelings because they surface during the moments of merriment or adversity. In other words, the way we fear the unknown determines the way we respond to life events. If we fear the unknown from a position of defeat, then we flee. But if we fear the unknown from the position of learning and discovery, then we can uncover the prison walls that once held our imaginations hostage. Every situation we face is always an angel in disguise. Our ability to embrace challenges of life rather than resenting them can bring an unending laughter to our situations and future.

So the next time you encounter a problem, remind yourself that it is an angel in disguise. Give the problem your undivided attention by focusing on the limitless, boundless opportunities such a problem can bring to your life if handled well.

Researchers Gregg Steinber and Lori Gano-Overway (2003) suggested the importance of applying explanatory style to our situations. In other words, the attitude to which we explain our problems makes a world of difference. I discuss three types of explanatory styles in this chapter.

1. Personalization style suggests that people who tend to internalize their problems by blaming the situation wholly on them are generally too hard on themselves. In other words, they failed to consider

other factors that could have contributed to the event. For example, in the case of Horatio Spafford, he could have blamed himself for allowing his family to travel without him and not suspending his business deal and following them. Instead, he thanked the Lord for at least saving his wife. In the midst of it all, he composed "It Is Well with My Soul." We easily blame ourselves when something terribly goes wrong, especially to somebody we love and care for, without even considering other possibilities. When we do this, we put unhealthy stress upon ourselves.

2. Permanence suggests that people tend to make monuments out of their problems. In other words, they perceived their problems to be long lasting and permanent. The issue about this approach is that we make that problem the center or part of our life without considering other possible ways of solving those problems. By implication, nothing is that permanent because life is constantly changing or growing. In the case of Horatio Spafford, he could have dwelled on the fact that his four beautiful daughters were gone forever as a result of his choice to stay back and finish his business deal in Chicago. And he could have chosen to stay in that space of mind forever, which would have gradually destroyed his own health and mental (psychological) state of mind. Instead, he expressed himself by composing a hymn.

3. Pervasiveness simply suggests whether the problem is universal or specific. After all, people lose their children all the time, accidents happen quite regularly, and businesses fail continually. Therefore, nothing can be that specific to the point that you are the only one who has ever experienced such tragedy. In other words, although the situation was tragic and painful, please understand that you are not alone. Others have experienced similar situations elsewhere. When we come to life with this kind of attitude, we tend to have a better chance of seeing our struggles for what they are without magnifying them.

So when you run into a problem, ask yourself what kind of fear you are experiencing and using to explain your situation: personalization explanatory, permanence, or pervasiveness? If you can get a grip of your fear by explaining what you are feeling and basing it on what you know, you can much more handle your fears from a constructive perspective as opposed to destructive. And you can learn how to forgive yourself and others when life situations occur.

The next chapter will tackle a familiar language called forgiveness and the way it applies to why people fear to forgive. Forgiveness is challenging because it is intangible and intrinsic. In other words, our internal environment determines whether to forgive or not. Forgiveness cannot be touched physically or tangibly, yet it has a strong hold on our intrapersonal and interpersonal relationships. As such, conversations that go on in our head compel us to outwardly express the method of approach when we are offended or violated—whether to hold grudges or not or to let go or withhold forgiveness.

For the moment while reading this chapter, suspend your personal biases about the subject, and approach it with an open mind, ready to see forgiveness from a different perspective. Before reading this chapter, write down your elementary understanding about forgiveness and the experiences you had prior to reading this chapter. After reading the chapter, give yourself some time to analyze what you have read, and ask yourself a series of questions. Who gains the most from forgiveness: the offender or the offended? Do you forgive others with conditions, or do you forgive others for you? What makes the most sense to you when you do forgive? Whatever responses you come out with, write them down as they appeared in your present space of mind. This note will help you remember how you once felt before and after reading this chapter.

Chapter 6

Why We Fear to Forgive Some People

Dr. Candice Pert, an internationally recognized pharmacologist, has published over 250 scientific articles on peptides and other receptors and other roles of these neuropeptides in the immune system. She served for many years as chief of brain biochemistry of the National Institute of Mental Health (NIMH) and said, "Forgiveness is a powerful weapon." It is the antidote for letting go the thoughts that sap our energy. Nobody could say it better than Dr. Candice Pert did.

This chapter will explore why we fear to forgive. Hopefully, it will help readers understand the benefits and urgency of forgiveness to both the offender and offended. We will explore one true story as a baseline for discussion. I will also use other research work to support this discussion on forgiveness.

It is reasonable to note that nobody of age has never been offended or wronged by friends, family members, colleagues, clients, and so forth. On the other hand, we have also wronged others in one fashion or another. Therefore, nobody is immune to this malady called incivility. Because we are all guilty of offending each other, why do we find it so difficult to forgive others when they offend us? We can come up with thousands and thousands of reasons and excuses why we cannot forgive one another. In truth, we are as guilty as the next person who will offend us the next minute.

To give life to this chapter, Cheryl and Jeff Scruggs wrote a book, *I Do Again: How We Found a Second Chance at Our Marriage—And You Can Too.* Cheryl and Jeff Scruggs, a very successful couple, fell in love and got married. They had material possessions but could not fulfill each other's emotional needs. As most men can attest to this, Jeff, a white-collar male, thought their marriage was great. On the other hand, Cheryl was feeling empty and lonely even though money was not the issue because they lived by the California beachfront with no children. They could literally afford good things in life.

Cheryl thought that having a baby could fill the void she was feeling, so they were blessed with beautiful twin daughters. Cheryl was still not happy, and her husband never knew her loneliness.

As a saleswoman for an office equipment company, she joined her company at a national sales meeting in Florida. While there, she met one of her male sales colleagues from the Northern California office, and they started talking at a dinner party on the last day. The conversation between Cheryl and her male colleague got personal as they started talking about their unhappy relationships with their partners. Although nothing happened between them in Florida, when they went back to California, their conversation became more intense as they spent hours over the phone.

Fortunately, Jeff got a new job in Texas. He was unaware of what was going on between Cheryl and her work colleague. Cheryl hoped that the relocation, leaving her colleague in California, could stop the emotional bond between them.

As fate might have it, Cheryl and her colleague were still keeping in touch for hours over the phone. Their emotional affair intensified to the point of her colleague flying to Texas to meet Cheryl, who then had an affair with her colleague. The rest was history. Cheryl's love grew stronger for her colleague to the point that she had no more feelings left for Jeff.

Without telling Jeff what was going on behind closed doors, she asked him for a divorce. A devastated Jeff could not figure out what really went wrong, and Cheryl never told him about the affair. Eventually, Cheryl served Jeff with divorce papers, and as soon as the divorce was final, Cheryl called her colleague out of excitement to tell him.

Throughout her love affair with her colleague, she was never at peace with herself. Still, Cheryl was free from Jeff and available for her colleague. A devastated Jeff kept his demeanor and faith. He became more spiritual and stronger in his faith.

Six and a half years after their divorce, Cheryl wrote an emotionally charged letter asking Jeff for forgiveness. This is where the rubber meets the road. What would Jeff do? Knowing what you know about Cheryl and Jeff's story, what would you do if you were in Jeff's shoes? This is a tough situation, knowing what Cheryl put Jeff through.

1. Cheryl deceived and lied to Jeff.
2. Cheryl betrayed Jeff.
3. Cheryl broke their covenant with God.

Learn to Forgive

According to Cheryl and Jeff Scruggses' story, as noted in their book, Jeff forgave Cheryl after seven long years of divorce. They renewed their vows, and they are living together as husband and wife. Their grown twin daughters have moved on in life. This could be nerve-racking to know that Jeff found a place in his heart to forgive Cheryl. What can we learn from Jeff and Cheryl's ordeal?

Researcher Michael Stone noted "our ability to appreciate the strengths admirable qualities in others and ourselves is reduced, discretionary effort is limited, and our ability to be fully present and focused on current issues and projects are greatly diminished" when we failed to forgive. By implication, we fear to forgive because we have an elusive mind-set that, if we forgive, we relinquish our strengths. Conversely, we relinquish our strengths if we do not forgive. In other words, we lack focus and sense of presence every time we encounter the person who wronged us and we fail to forgive him or her. It is a toxic exercise not to forgive. When we fail to forgive, it has a spillover effect even in the workplace. Evidently, forgiveness supports retention-valued employees; allows for creativity and innovation, which leads to increased profitability; and provokes higher flexibility in adapting to changing market conditions (Stone 2005). Forgiveness in the workplace increases organizational growth and healthy living because we all experience spillover effect. In other words, what happens in the workplace affects our relationships with our children, wives, and even our friends. Therefore, walking with grudges is unhealthy and depreciates quality of life as we carry the stress of unforgiveness.

Researcher Beth Shapiro noted that forgiveness should not just be perceived as a spiritual cleansing but also as a physical and emotional well-being. Evidently, forgiveness is most useful to that person who forgives and not for the forgiven. In other words, unforgiveness is an act of welcoming unhealthy behavior and an exercise of spiritual suicide because unforgiveness is a silent killer. It systematically equips a person with grudges, hatred, maliciousness, and so forth. These are all toxic energies.

C. Philpot from University of Queensland, Brisbane, Australia, supported the notion that forgiveness aids psychological healing through positive changes in effect. This means that, when we forgive, it carries a seed of positive change and heals the offended psychologically, a psychological healing that allows you to live life to the fullest with no regrets. The Bible makes several references about forgiveness and its benefits (Matt. 6:12; Luke 11:4, 6:37, 23:34). These cited Bible chapters are evidence that forgiveness has a boomerang effect. By forgiving others, you are essentially positioning yourself to be forgiven by others because it is inevitable that you will offend somebody someday. Therefore, we should not fear to forgive others. Rather, we should anticipate to forgive when people offend us. That anticipation to forgive should push us to constructively fear to forgive. Remember, constructive fear is a healthy fear. It has a positive outcome. Take, for example, the story of the Good Samaritan in the Bible.

In the case of the Good Samaritan, fear caused the priest, the Levite, and the Samaritan to have acted the way they did when they found a wounded person by the roadside. In other words, fear provokes you to either act or respond. You act when you fail to thoroughly process information or the situation at hand. Conversely, you respond when you think through the consequences and inconsequence of failure to act.

In the next chapter, we will explore the bystander effect, one that speaks on how people respond or react to situations in public using the Good Samaritan approach to make a case. Before you help somebody in public, do you consider certain factors such as environment, relationship, "save face" attitude, or consequences of not helping? Can you assist a stranger the same way you help an individual you know, whether in a private or public place? What determines how you assist a person? We subconsciously go through these questions on a daily basis. The intent of the next chapter is to create awareness and suggest certain principles that could help relieve our fears when we are in a position of assisting others.

Chapter 7

The Good Samaritan

Social psychologist Melissa Burkley, PhD, at Oklahoma State University, noted that people are reluctant to help in public, especially when a few of them witness the same situation. For example, on October 24, 2009, as many as twenty witnesses watched as a fifteen-year-old was brutally assaulted and raped outside a homecoming dance in Richmond, California. As brutal as it sounds, some bystanders were laughing and taking pictures of the event with their cell phones. This behavior raised a question why that many people would fail to help the fifteen-year-old. Such cases have happened in several other cities with similar reactions.

- In 2005, a twenty-two-year-old college student died from water intoxication when four of his fellow fraternity brothers failed to intervene during a deadly hazing incident.
- In 1964, twenty-eight-year-old Kitty Genovese was raped and stabbed to death in the Kew Gardens neighborhood of Queens, New York, while several

dozen people witnessed the rape and did nothing to stop it.

- In New Bedford, Massachusetts, in 1983, several men raped a woman on a pool table in front of witnesses in a bar without urgent reaction to that incident.

The list is endless. If these incidents seem strange to you, have you ever witnessed a vehicle break down or catch on fire on a busy freeway and assume that somebody must have called 9-1-1 to help? Or you went to a nightclub for fun and witnessed a fistfight between two guys inside the club. Instead of calling security or help, you either joined others to watch the fight or quietly left the scene.

If you have experienced any of these cases, why did you feel reluctant to help or call for help? Every one of us wrestles with these questions, and we probably have a thousand reasons why we failed to help. Social psychologist Melissa Burkley, PhD, suggested that, when others on the scene of the incident did not treat it as an emergency, chances are, more people felt reluctant to do something, fearing others on the scene knew more than they did about the incident or they wanted to avoid looking foolish. By implication, we could see this untested assumption as destructive fear because we failed to respond. A constructive fear approach would suggest that we respond accordingly, knowing what could happen to the victim if we didn't react.

Even students tend to have similar situations in a classroom when a professor is teaching a topic about something they do not understand. One student struggling to understand the lecture happens to have a question. If he or she looks around the room and sees that nobody raises a hand to ask a question, to avoid looking stupid, the student is likely to keep his or her hand down, dying in silence.

In this instance, the right fear to have is constructive fear, asking, *If I do not ask this question, how would I learn?* Instead, the student might go home in silence, whereby losing an opportunity to learn new information. In this scenario, such student has just demonstrated destructive fear, one that will deter him or her from knowing what he or she ought to know. In case you noticed what was going on with that student, will you reach out to encourage him or her? Or will you assume that some other students could help? For you to respond differently, ask yourself, *If I do not encourage the student to speak up, what will happen to him or her in the future?*

Chances are, such behavior will perpetuate, and the student will quietly be dying in fear of being ridiculed. There is a need for us to step up for somebody who needs our help; else, we will perpetuate this issue of bystander effect (standing by watching and doing nothing to help). There is a biblical illustration where we can learn a great deal about this lesson. On this premise, this chapter is titled the Good Samaritan.

Bystander Effect from Different Perspectives

In Luke 10:29–37, a certain lawyer asked Jesus, "And who is my neighbor?" And Jesus told him a parable of the Good Samaritan, saying,

> "A certain man went down from Jerusalem to Jericho, and fell among thieves, who stripped him of his clothing, wounded him, and departed, leaving him half dead. Now by chance a certain priest came down that road. And when he saw him, he passed by on the other side. Likewise a Levite, when he arrived at the place, came and looked, and passed by on the other side. But a certain Samaritan, as he journeyed, came where he was. And when he saw him, he had compassion. So he went to him and bandaged his wounds, pouring on oil and wine: and he set him on his own animal, brought him to an inn, and took care of him. On the next day, when he departed, he took out two denarii, gave them to the inn-keeper, and said to him, 'Take care of him; and whatever more you spend, when I come again, I will repay you.'"

So Jesus asked the lawyer, "So which of these three do you think was neighbor to him who fell among the thieves?"

And the lawyer answered, "He who showed mercy on him."

This parable has so many lessons to teach us, but for the sake of this chapter and the theme of the book, let's talk about those three bystanders—the priest, the Levite, and the Samaritan—from fear perspectives. Notice that all three of them feared but from different scopes.

- The first individual (the priest) feared, "If I helped the wounded man, what would happen to me, me, me?" Maybe he was in a hurry (like all of us claim to be); therefore, he did not want to be bothered with additional burden. In this context, his fear was destructive because he ignored the urgency of helping the wounded man; further, he ignored the fact that one of his spiritual obligations was to serve others. Unfortunately, the loudspeakers of his conscience were broken at that particular moment. What does his behavior teach us about his position as a moral leader?
- The second person was a Levite. We can also conclude that he had something to do; therefore, he did not want to be bothered.
- The third person, the Samaritan, probably had something to do as well, but he asked himself, *If I do not help this wounded man, what would happen to him?* Just by asking that simple but powerful question, he was provoked to help the wounded man. In this case, he had a constructive fear that, if

he failed to help the wounded man, he could bleed to death. That thought compelled him to maximize every resource he had to make sure the wounded man was taken care of.

Can we take a moment and analyze these three men's behaviors toward the wounded man? Have we played any of those roles at some point in our lives, those of nonchalant attitude, aloofness, and distance? On the other hand, have we asked, *If I fail to help them, what would happen to them?* It is a social phenomenon. Association for Psychological Science Fellow Joseph Ferrari, professor of psychology at DePaul University, noted in his research that as many as 20 percent of people may be chronic procrastinators, persistent in the sense that it has become a habit.

To apply it in this scenario, people have a 20 percent chance of not doing something as a result of procrastination, thereby pushing the most tedious tasks by the side and settling for the less demanding tasks. In the case of helping the wounded man, it was obviously a time-consuming and emotionally demanding task; therefore, 20 percent of people will avoid doing the right thing in this context. As an avenue of creating awareness, would you rather be on the 20 percent who will not help or the 80 percent who will do something to help? It is a personal question that requires thorough reflection and conscious effort to make a shift in thinking. That is, if you are the one who needs help, would you expect people to help you or to procrastinate helping you?

To further support the issue of procrastination and the way it relates to the subject in discussion, Timothy Pychyl of Carleton University, Canada, noted that procrastinators recognize the temporal harm in what they are doing, but they can't overcome the emotional urge toward a diversion. In other words, procrastination is a deliberate action with emotional urge attached to it. Even though the current situation at hand is urgent, a procrastinator will still postpone current action to focus on something of lesser importance. Therefore, the common denominator in this instance is fear, be it constructive or destructive.

Now that we have scratched the surface on the subject of the Good Samaritan, helping others in any circumstance is determined by the kind of fear we are operating on at that particular moment and based on memorized emotions (how we normally respond to similar situations). In other words, being conscious of what we fear and why we fear it is a safe way of putting our fears in check, especially when we come to a situation to help others. We should examine our fears by asking a simple question: *If I fail to help people who are in dangerous situations, what will happen to them?* Our internal environment to that question determines our next course of action. Relatively observing our internal environment determines the quality of our fears, suggesting that fear has different qualities in the sense of low- and high-quality fears.

The next chapter will address different qualities of fear, specifically in the sense of decision-making as it relates to the workplace and the academic environment. We will attempt to draw from practical life experiences and examples to suggest that fear does have qualities. Please note that we are not discussing fear in terms of dangerous circumstances such as emergency situations. Rather, it's from a position of normalcy and everyday encounters. By all means, we should handle emergency situations as urgently as possible. It cannot be compromised.

Hopefully, this chapter will shed positive light on how we come to terms with fear when it relates to workplaces, relationships, and academic environments—that is, our most vulnerable spaces. These are areas of vulnerability to people on a regular basis. Therefore, examine the quality of your fears. That way, you will make sound decisions.

Chapter 8

The Quality of Fear

Quality is associated with long-lasting impression, durability, healthy choices, and so forth. In most cases, quality is associated with values. If the value of a product or decision is impactful and carries longevity, it is usually coined to be high quality and expensive in monetary terms as well. In other words, quality decisions or products require some processes, creative thinking, or research, or it simply implies that it is time consuming. In most situations, for decisions we value, we tend to make them thoroughly and with precision. On the other hand, people who engage in unhealthy situations do so out of peer pressure or hasty conclusions, or they're simply instantaneous. As a result, they produce poor quality and judgment at the expense of saving face, playing good guy, and so forth.

For example, consider organic food products, which are usually expensive because of the quality and processes taken to arrive at the final product. Growing spinach organically means taking natural processes—that is, planting it in the ground using as few chemicals as possible (with preferably no chemicals at all) to grow it and waiting for the germination and maturity processes to take its course. In the end, spinach grown organically tastes much better and healthier than the one grown with chemicals. Because of following the natural process in growing organic spinach, it is more expensive for purchase.

Using these analogies, we can relate them to qualities of fear as well because some fears are unhealthy while some are healthy. Unhealthy fear can be coined as a low-quality fear while healthy fear is coined as high quality. Both took time to produce, but high-quality fears take more time, along with critical and creative thinking, to produce. The concepts are applicable to other areas of engagements.

Workplace and Fear

Don McCallum, a retired minister who continues to serve part time at St. Andrew's United and St. Mary's Anglican Church in Lillooet, British Columbia, Canada, noted, "Whatever our fears, they can be immobilizing and unhealthy if we dwell on them very long—or exaggerate them. Fears can be healthy, however, if they lead us to take constructive action." In other words, healthy fears can lead to constructive actions and produce high-quality results.

In his experience, Don McCallum shared at the age of nineteen that he started smoking, but after two years, he realized that smoking started to irritate his tongue and dull his taste. Most importantly, he started to notice that, in his cross-country skiing around a fifteen-kilometer course, he was getting slower instead of faster. This shift in his behavior disturbed him because he planned to participate on his university's team. With the rate he was going (slower and slower), his dream of participating at the university was becoming unattainable if he continued his smoking habit.

Because of his thorough analysis of himself, he quit smoking at the age of twenty-one. Evidently, his constructive fear allowed him to give up smoking and focus on training for cross-country skiing. In this context, his fear of not being able to attain his skiing dream brought him to a place of high-quality fear. Obviously, we can trade our low-quality fear for a high-quality one by engaging in critical and positive thinking processes—no matter the setting, whether in relationships, academic environments, or workplaces.

Barton Goldsmith, PhD, an award-winning psychotherapist, business consultant, author, speaker, and syndicated columnist, stated that, in the workplace, fear dwarfs our productivity, communications, ability to create, and emotional well-being. By implication, identifying and acknowledging that we have fear in our system is the first step to healing. What we fear is also critical to know because knowing is empowering. It allows us to decide the course of action. Our approach to reverse those negative effects that fear contributes in the workplace is a recipe for high-quality fear. In this context, we have allowed fear to expose us to a solution of peace and confidence. When this happens, fear has become of high quality. On the other hand, when we dwell in our pains and negativisms (that is, poor communication skills, inability to create, and unstable emotional well-being), we operate on a low-quality fear. So pay attention to what kind of result we are anticipating and feeling. This will help us change our course of action from low-quality fear to high-quality fear.

Let's apply a typical workplace fear scenario. Your workload increased by 10 percent. Because of the increase, you started working longer hours. Your supervisor approached you on the issue of allowed overtime. In other words, you are working too many hours not justified by the increase of your workload. You tried explaining the reasons for overtime to your supervisor, but your supervisor still insisted. Specifically:

1. If you fail to constructively articulate your reasons with statistical evidence to your supervisor, chances are, you will start to fear losing your job, and you will worry about what will happen to your job on a daily basis. Eventually, your fear will reflect on your productivity and communications, and ultimately, your feelings will start to fluctuate. Doubt, anger, pretense, and so forth, will start to surface. Unfortunately, your performance will spiral.

2. If you don't change your thinking pattern in regard to that situation, you will fall victim to the very thing you fear. So go back to the drawing board and ask yourself, *Am I communicating my reasons clearly?*

Am I still concentrating undividedly to my job tasks? And am I still producing? If your supervisor still does not respond to your explanations, chances are, you have not sold your points to him or her. Pay attention to those nonverbal languages because they speak volumes.

Barton Goldsmith, PhD, further stated that, in order to deal with our situations in the workplace, we need to start talking about them. In other words, don't beat around the bush. Be specific when you articulate your points. Mind your words. Make sure that what you are saying is relevant to what is at hand. Don't assume that your supervisor knows the problem. Chances are, he or she might know from his or her own perspective. It is up to you to make your case with evidence and not emotions. Conversely, your supervisor should also make it safe for you to be able to express your position. If your supervisor does not provide such an environment, ask that he or she do. It is your right to feel safe in the workplace; therefore, don't worry about your supervisor shutting you down.

Remember, articulate your points, and give your supervisor time to respond. When you apply these principles and notice a collaborative result, then you have produced a high-quality result because of high-quality fear. The same principles apply between students and professors or between students.

Academics and Fear

In the academic journey, students who survive or graduate are not necessarily the smartest of all students. Rather, those students stayed the test of time. They understand that completing a project requires not only effort but also persistence in the face of obstacles so they do not abandon the task.

Angela Lee Duckworth, an assistant professor of psychology at the University of Pennsylvania and a colleague, emphasized that enormous talent is no guarantee of grit (courage, endurance, or success). Instead, her experiment suggested that talented people are, on average, less gritty (less courageous). Therefore, it is rare to see people who are gritty and talented at the same time.

What distinguishes a person from the other is his or her ability to stay on task even in times of obvious difficulties. Angela Duckworth and her colleagues used prospective longitudinal studies to draw their conclusions. Longitudinal study is where a researcher follows a group of participants for a long period of time, whereby recording participants' activities. At the end of the study, he or she will report or document his or her findings. For example, not all of the smartest students in their first year in college usually complete their four-year degree program. Instead, some of those students with mediocre GPAs but determination to graduate have better chances of graduating. In other words, passing all the entry-level exams with flying colors, demonstrating talent, and having strong predictions of academic success are not the qualities that predict retention. This means that some students may start with minimal qualifications but have grittier attitude toward life. They would likely sustain the test of time if they studied harder and stayed on the race.

Comparatively, whether you are a talented or mediocre student, the only language that guarantees success is to those who view life as if it were a marathon, not a sprint. When you view academic challenges from this scope, you will experience high-quality fear, one that yields constructive action. Therefore, if you are not doing well in your academic pursuit, don't entertain low-quality fear. Rather, keep studying hard, and stay on track.

Dr. Benjamin Carson, chief pediatric neurosurgeon at Johns Hopkins Hospital in Baltimore, shared his academic struggles when his academic counselor told him that he was not intelligent enough to handle the pressure needed for academic excellence. His academic counselor based his decision on the fact that Benjamin Carson was not doing too well during his school years. But because he was determined, committed, and gritty (courageous), he stayed on track and graduated from Yale and University of Michigan. His academic journey supports the notion that life is not a sprint but a marathon. That is, it's not when you start that matters. It's if you indeed finish the race.

American Psychological Association reported that students from low-income families dropped out of high school five times more frequently than students from high-income families in 2009—and poverty is the link for such a high school dropout. African American students represented 45 percent of dropouts nationally compared to 34 percent for white males. The US Department of Education reported this in 2007. One of the reasons of such a high dropout rate among African American males was their erroneous assumption (fear) that their employment and financial status outcomes would be identical regardless of whether they graduated high school or not. Therefore, many African American males drop out of the race prematurely. This stat indicates low-quality fear.

Irrespective of race or gender, we should be able to encourage any person who finds himself or herself in this position of low-quality fear and educate him or her to understand that dropping out of high school has serious socioeconomic damages.

Facts about African American High School Dropout Males

- African American high school dropouts essentially have problems securing jobs, whereby creating negative effects on the community and levying financial burdens on social and welfare programs.
- Dropping out of high school increases the risk for unemployment, poverty, drug and substance abuse, and even discrimination among African American males compared to those who completed high school (Lowe 2010).

- It also increases the risk of being incarcerated and often promotes negative stereotypes of African American males (Lowe 2010, 8).

Other races and genders can face similar deficiencies as African American high school dropout males do. This economic and social handicap affects every human who fits within the scopes as described in this text. To turn the tide to a different direction, high-quality fear is critical. In other words, one should ask, *If I drop out of high school, I have positioned myself to face all the calamities and more listed above.* So don't be a victim of information. Be a creator of positive energy, and act sooner rather than later.

We have learned how fear has qualities: high quality, low quality, healthy, and unhealthy. Fear is a natural phenomenon. Nobody is immune to it. Rather, we can only prepare ourselves to entertain fear.

But we face another challenge, fear of rejection. Have we ever feared rejection either by a friend, stranger, job, date, school, society, and so forth? The answer to these questions should be a resounding yes because fear of rejection is part of human nature. Sometimes we reject others and feel no remorse about it, but when we are rejected, we tend to be devastated. In some cases, we ask, *Why me?* Well, why not you? If it's not you, who? We need to learn how to develop a thick skin by accepting rejection as a way of life because fear of rejection has a mysterious strength. Rejection can provoke someone to overcome obstacles, or it can demoralize a person. The choice is yours because you are the only person who really has most to do with what happens to you.

The next chapter challenges our social biases and emotional intelligence. In other words, it challenges our make-believe and forces us to reserve judgment and ask questions. Am I perfect? Is my way the only way? How much do I know? In fact, could what I know be limited to my exposure and routines? We will attempt to address these questions. Be your own referee while I will be the hand that writes. Hopefully, you will be able to challenge what you already know and allow new information to guide your views about life.

Chapter 9

Fear of Rejection

Steven M. Southwick, MD, professor of psychiatry at Yale School of Medicine, and Dennis S. Charney, MD, dean and professor of psychiatry, neuroscience, pharmacology, and systems therapeutics at the Mount Sinai School of Medicine, in *Resilience: The Science of Mastering Life's Greatest Challenges*, noted, "Fear is constricting and even paralyzing, while for others it is energizing and serves as a catalyst for growth." In their attempt to explain how relevant fear is in our lives, they cited Nelson Mandela's words on fear:

> I learned that courage was not the absence of fear, but the triumph over it. I felt fear myself more times than I can remember, but I hid it behind the mask of boldness. The brave man is not he who does not feel afraid, but he who conquers that fear.

Evidently, fear is no respecter of persons. Great people admit being afraid. Even his own South African government rejected Nelson Mandela because of his fight for equality in South Africa. He spent over twenty-five years of his life in jail for a good cause. Imagine the emotions going through his mind while in jail, yet he triumphed and became the first black president of the Republic of South Africa in 1994.

Several brave men and women admitted being afraid in the midst of their struggles, but they persevered and turned their fear of rejection into an opportunity. Therefore, rejection is not denial. Neither is it the end of life. Rather, it is the beginning of a new dawn and horizon because rejection reminds us that we are humans with feelings. Every rejection should be an opportunity to demonstrate the awesomeness of our creator.

This chapter will further present women and men who experienced rejection to the core and yet overcame the emotional challenges associated with rejection. Today, they are at peace with themselves for facing the giant of fear of rejection by taking constructive actions rather than entertaining destructive fear of rejection.

A Graduate Facing Unemployment Challenges

Patience Akpan-Obong, a student and a Nigerian national with restricted work authorization schooling in Canada, was pursuing her master's degree in journalism. This degree program would have taken two years, but she completed it in one year with intensity and dedication in 1996. Upon completion of her degree program, her summer job at the *Ottawa Citizen* ended as well. With pressure to secure the next job, she reported submitting at least two hundred applications within a one-month period but to no avail. Even advertised positions were suddenly filled as soon as she called to make enquiries, yet those positions were still available for hiring. This kind of experience is enough to make a new graduate like Ms. Patience regret pursuing an advanced degree. It will even create an emotional feeling as fear of rejection. It is a space where certainty becomes an illusion. It's the great promise that life should improve for us when we graduate from university life.

But that was not the case for Ms. Patience. As if that experience were not enough, one of her former professors heard about a new job opening at a government agency and notified Ms. Patience to apply for the position. The government agency was looking for a qualified candidate who could create Internet-based programs for schools across the country. Ms. Patience's former professor felt she was qualified for the position, so she sent a compelling letter of recommendation to the director of the government agency recommending Ms. Patience for the position. Ms. Patience applied for the position and attached her master's research project that tackled challenges that online newspapers presented for the traditional print newspaper. Upon receipt, the director was impressed with her work and invited her for an interview.

When Ms. Patience arrived for the interview, the director suddenly acted indifferently by not making any eye contact or asking questions that showed a high level of interest to hire Ms. Patience. Needless to say, the director claimed she was overqualified for the position. Yet the director was willing to hire her to work ten hours a week at ten dollars an hour. As if that were not enough stress, Ms. Patience, out of curiosity, told the interviewer that she would accept the offer. The director then asked her to submit her complete master's research project because she would like to use it as a training tool for her staff. Understandably, Ms. Patience never heard from the interviewer; neither did she go back to that office to accept the offer.

From these two experiences, Ms. Patience really had struggles that would have qualified her to throw in the towel and conclude in her mind that she was not good for anything. Evidently, such a claim would have created an emotion of fear of rejection. But Ms. Patience took a different and constructive course of action to her dilemma.

She went ahead to pursue her PhD in political science, a journey that concluded in 2003 at the University of Alberta, Canada. Currently, Dr. Patience Akpan-Obong is an associate professor of science, technology, and society in the School of Letters and Sciences at Arizona State University's Polytechnic, Mesa, Arizona. She shared her stories in her second book, *Letters to Nigeria: Journal of an African Woman in America.* Dr. Patience is happily married and lives in Arizona with her family. What is the relevance of her story?

Fear of rejection can either erode your morale, confidence, hope, and so forth, or it can propel you into a new imagination and new reality. In Dr. Patience's case, she chose to use her rejections to reach a new height. Her triumph over her life challenges ought to be a motivational tool for students who think it is impossible to excel in the face of difficulties or who think rejection means denial. The choice is yours. Rejection can be whatever you want it to be because fear of rejection transcends race, classism, sexism, religion, gender, or sexual orientation. Therefore, it does not matter whether you are in politics, academics, or business or are young, old, straight, or gay. The heat of fear of rejection echoes across the globe. As long as you have breath inside of you, an iota of fear of rejection is in you. The only difference is how you see yourself and your problems—never ending or temporary. How do we overcome fear of rejection?

Five Steps to Overcome Fear of Rejection

Have a Clear Goal

A study conducted by psychologists Dominique Morisano, PhD, at the Child and Family Institute, St. Luke's-Roosevelt Hospital Center, New York; Jordan B. Peterson, PhD, at the University of Toronto, Canada; Jacob Hirsh, a postdoctoral student at the University of Toronto, Canada; and Robert O. Pihl and Bruce M. Shore from McGill University shows that 25 percent of university students who enroll in a four-year university program never graduate. Major causes of early departure are poor academic progress and lack of clear goals and motivation. The same study suggested that "clearly defined and articulated goals give people purpose and meaning and protect them from anxiety and despair." Therefore, there is a relationship between lack of clear goal and anxiety (fear). Evidently, if an individual has goal clarity, chances are, the level of anxiety will reduce, and morale will increase.

To apply this concept in our discussion about Dr. Patience, her second rejection happened when she was finally called with the help of her former professor writing a profound letter of recommendation to the director who later confirmed that Dr. Patience's résumé was impressive and invited her to interview. The interviewer decided she was overqualified; therefore, she would not be hired unless she would accept a job making one hundred dollars a week. And she was also asked to send in her master's research project so the interviewer's boss could use it for staff training. Notwithstanding the rejections and humiliation, Dr. Patience went back to the university and obtained her PhD from the University of Alberta, Canada. Her courageous move indicates that she had a clear goal; therefore, she did not allow fear of rejection to handicap her goal.

Think about Dr. Patience's dilemma, and contemplate when you found yourself in a similar situation. How did you handle it? Did you reaffirm your goal, or did you give up your quest for greatness? Fear of rejection should not be a crutch to our failure. Rather, it should be a step to our new height. The application of fear of rejection should work in other settings—relationships, workplaces, or life in general. Your problems must obey your destiny if you have a clear goal and believe in yourself.

Do you think that a high divorce rate is a result of distorted goals between a couple? Do you think that an employee who quits his or her job because of stress could be the result of a distorted shift in his or her initial goal about the organization? A friends' separation is because the thread that holds the friendship was distorted by an event that both individuals failed to clearly redefine their friendship. A student drops out of college because of a distorted goal.

Therefore, if we can clearly define our goal, chances are, we will attain such an achievement. Though it may tarry, if we don't give in to the pressures of life, we shall overcome whatever obstacle we encounter. All you need is a rebirth of your vision—that is, putting your vision in front of you rather than behind you.

Change Your Memorized Emotions about Fear

Possibly, most of the emotions associated with fear are negative. This means we only hear about fear when something negative is about to happen or is going on. For example:

- Students preparing for exams confide in their friends about their fears of failing the exams.

- During a national economic crisis, a human resources manager calls for an all-staff meeting. The staff fears that the reason for the meeting is that the company could be downsizing. One of the employees verbalizes that everyone is thinking about downsizing. More people would fear just because they already have a fear of losing their jobs.

The list is endless. Because of these memorized emotions, whenever new information is presented, we tend to refer to a similar situations, and as a result, we fear such repeating itself. This type of mental attitude creates unhealthy stress. But can we erase this fear of rejection in our minds?

Psychiatrists Steven M. Southwick and Dennis S. Charney noted that "focusing excessively on potential negative or catastrophic scenarios can be harmful because precious time and resources are wasted fretting about the unknown." Therefore, replacing the unknown with the known would help the situation. In this case, the known is that you are alive and well. You have made it this far in life without dying. You have, at one time in your life, overcome an obstacle, no matter how small. Most importantly, you are a human being; therefore, humans experience difficulties every now and then, and you are no different. Dr. Maya Angelou, whom Alexander Choman described as one of the greatest writers of our time, once said, "I am a human being. Nothing human can be alien to me" (Eaton 1994). Dr. Maya Angelou borrowed this quote from a Roman slave named Terence, whom a Roman senator bought. He was noted for writing six plays and became a favorite in Roman literary circles. This freed slave profoundly believed in the power of his being despite incredible odds.

What's the lesson to be learned from this slave? If a slave believed in the power of being even in the face of humiliation and captivity, is your case worse than a slave that you can believe in the power of being? In this context, replace your fear of rejection with the fact that difficulties are meant for humans and humans are powerful beings; therefore, human spirits cannot be broken without their permission. Memorize this emotion, and remember it each time you feel like your life is worse than anybody in the world. If you can change your thoughts, you can change your world.

Surround Yourself with Diverse Minds

We have heard the saying, "Iron sharpens iron." This means that the circumstances you are facing cannot be solved with lower or equal level of ideas. Therefore, surround yourself with people who positively intimidate you, those who have the solutions and ideas you are looking for or the place and space where you are going in terms of goals and vision. When you do this, you will learn how they are overcoming their fears and how you can make fear your best friend, especially fear of rejection. Fear of rejection reminds you that you are human, and only in rejection can we learn how to overcome fear of rejection.

According to the Bureau of Labor Statistics latest data on workers as of 2012 who are now between the ages of forty-six and fifty-four, the average member of that group has had 11.3 jobs in his or her lifetime, and men switch jobs more than women do (Belser 2012). The researcher used longitudinal survey to collect data. This means that the same group of people was followed in this case from 1979 to 1994 and every other year since then. Using this information to draw a contrast on fear of rejection suggests that this group of people had numerous jobs before they turned fifty-four years of age. It is fair to say that they must have experienced rejection at work numerous times as well. So people who survive life struggles are aware that rejection is inevitable. That is why it is important to surround yourself with people who have experienced and overcome what you fear.

For you to learn from experienced folks, you must learn how to ask specific questions and avoid asking general questions. For example, you wanted to ask your friend who has experienced numerous fears of rejection a question about how it feels to be rejected at work so many times. You said, "Losing a job is not for everyone because it happens to people who don't know their jobs." This comment is an open-and-shut statement. This means the other person may choose to say nothing because you did not pose a question. Rather, it was a statement. The right approach will be, "I heard losing a job can happen to anyone" or "How do you normally deal with fear of rejection, especially when it's work related?" Now you are letting the other person chose how to answer the question in a conversational manner. In the process, you can learn a lot from the response.

You can gain knowledge from listening and talking with people who have experienced what you are going through or what you know is an unavoidable situation in life—for example, job loss. Equipping yourself with knowledge about a particular subject will increase your confidence and morale and prepare you on how to handle fear of rejection. Therefore, position yourself to learn from people who are experienced in whatever area you lack knowledge.

Cognitively Test the New You

Now that we have associated ourselves and learned from people who have overcome fear of rejection, we add new information in our memories. This means, each time we run into similar situations instead of using our old way of responding to fear, we now recollect the new way of responding to fear of rejection. Over time, our minds will automatically start to remind us how to respond to similar issues. Scholars call it cognitive scripts.

Juan Lucariello, PhD, professor of psychology and education psychology at City University of New York, noted that students come to school with considerable knowledge, some correct and some not. Intuition, everyday life, and what he or she had been taught in other settings shapes this knowledge. Therefore, when students show up in school, they come with preconceptions, which are what they live by. It is to both students and professors' advantage to find out what preconceptions students are bringing to the school. Based on such information, professors would build on their preconceptions as related to their respective disciplines. That process of reprogramming the students or adding to their established notions will help mold them to become better people in the future.

In this case, we can test our new information by testing our cognitive scripts. For example, there is an intern position open at a Semiconductor Company for software engineering students, and you would really like to work for them, but you feared your GPA was not 4.0 and you had no track record in your field. Your old thinking pattern would suggest that you should not waste your time applying because this Semiconductor Company would not hire a novice like you. Apply your new self by saying to yourself, *This company really wants novices like me to train. That was why the position was posted for interns; therefore, that qualifies me to apply.*

Just by overriding that negative thought, you are on your way to using fear of rejection to work for you. Similar scenarios such as relationships, work-related issues, and so forth, are examples of situations you can apply to new cognitive scripts to work for you. When you start processing constructive fear of rejection long enough in your mind, you will then start to build confidence and courage to act on it.

Act

Action is the interpreter of thoughts. Now that you have gained confidence and courage, you can apply yourself to situations you have discussed with your mentors and processed in your mind. For example, you can now drive to the Semiconductor Company building and submit a résumé for that software engineering intern position, knowing that the Semiconductor HR might invite you for an interview. But even if you were not called, that's okay; at least your résumé is in their file for the next twelve months, which means you can call them frequently to follow up with your application. Chances are, they can still call you when another opening is available.

This chapter has presented a great deal of information on how we can turn fear of rejection to work in our favor. Dr. Patience did it, and it worked for her. She did not allow her experiences with job hunting to cripple her goals. Rather, she rose above it by completing her PhD in political science and relocating to Arizona. Therefore, she is an epitome of courage.

The former president of South Africa, Nelson Mandela, shared his insight about fear and the way he viewed fear as an opportunity and a necessity of life. Other evidence-based studies and life experiences were used to support this chapter. So ask yourself, *Do I fear rejection as a tool to overcome life challenges, or do I view fear of rejection as a handicap to my existence?*

Chapter 10

The Inconvenient Truth

This chapter will attempt to address some issues that are controversial in our nation and across the globe for decades. The controversial nature of these issues provoked the author to choose the chapter title. Scientific studies and theological perspectives are the basis of support to allow readers to make their own decisions in such a way that education and new imagination is promoted. Hopefully, removing grudges, biases, rage, hatred, and judgmental behaviors toward this inconvenient truth will bring healing and wholeness to self.

These issues were coined "inconvenient truth" because societies have frowned upon them for decades, but the number of cases continues to increase in such a pace that is unavoidably noticeable from classrooms to boardrooms and from government official homes to religious settings. The message remains the same and universal. Significant shifts in thoughts toward the issues are increasing as an indication of change. However, to what extent do we allow this change, and how has this change either directly or indirectly affected our well-being? In other words, by embracing the fact that no force in universe can stop the movement, resistance to change continues to provoke negative energies from both parties, people in favor of the movement and those against it.

The question remains. How many people in America can claim they do not have a friend, family member, customer, client, and so forth, that belongs to the lesbian, gay, bisexual, and transgender (LGBT) community? Several studies support the fact that a significant amount of people know at least one person in their lives who belongs to this community. But yet as a society, we are repressing the fact and pretending that the impact on society is not noticeable or significant.

The second issue to be addressed in this chapter is the issue of violence in the United States and the world. It is escalating at an alarming rate, yet we are finding it difficult to accept the fact that whatever we are doing to reduce violence has not equated to the rate violence is increasing. Several scientific studies and cases demonstrate the magnitude of this issue of violence against humanity. These issues (LGBT and violence against humanity) are the themes of the chapter as it relates to fear.

Evidently, fear of the unknown holds us back from acknowledging the inconvenient truth. In truth, the human mind, as relating to sexual orientation, cannot be regulated. Instead, it can be closely observed for us to live a life of fulfillment.

Additionally, using force to solve human's inhumanity to man has never resolved any issue in life. Dr. Martin Luther King Jr., Mahatma Gandhi, Nelson Mandela,

Mother Teresa, and many more have proven that an eye for an eye leaves everyone blind. Therefore, approaching the issue of violence from evidence-based studies would create a better avenue for solution than distancing and using force to solve the issues of life. In order to maintain consistency, we will address the inconvenient truth about the LGBT community.

Fear of Dealing with the Inconvenient Truth

We fail to accept the truth in certain situations. For example, fifteen-year-old Amber came home from school and saw elderly men and women gathered in her house. Without understanding what was going on, as she approached her house, she felt negative emotions and a sense of grief on everybody's face. Instantly, she knew that somebody had died in her house. She took off running to nowhere because she did not want to hear who it could be. When her cousins finally brought her home, she realized her mother had passed. She got sick for several days, fighting the truth and pains of losing her mother. Imagine the emotional stress that was associated with the loss. Such pains can bring hurt to your soul, and a feeling of refusing to accept the experience followed after accepting the truth.

LGBT community members associated such grief of losing their loved ones to the feelings they felt when society feared to accept them for who they were. The Massachusetts Department of Public Health reported that, as a result of legal recognition of same-sex marriage in Massachusetts, 72 percent felt more committed to their partners, and 70 percent felt more accepted by their communities. In addition, 93 percent of children with same-sex parents reported feeling happier and better off.

But several states in the United States still fear to accept the truth that the stigma associated with the LGBT community is counterproductive. A study conducted by researchers Deborah Azrael, PhD, director of Research at Harvard Youth Violence Prevention Center; Renee M. Johnson, PhD, MPH, a research associate with the Harvard Youth Violence Prevention Center; Beth E. Molnar, an assistant professor of society, human development, and health at Harvard School of Public Health; Joanna Almeida, ScD, postdoctoral fellow at the Institute on Urban Health Research at Northeastern University; and Heather L. Corliss, PhD, MPH, instructor of pediatrics at Harvard Medical School and a research scientist at Children Hospital Boston, stated that 40 percent of youth who reported a minority sexual orientation indicated feeling sad and hopeless. Evidently, 40 percent of those studied participants who felt sad and hopeless socialized with other kids on a daily basis. Imagine what kind of negative vibes (sadness and hopelessness) they are injecting around as a result of other people's inability to accept them for who they are.

Over time, such emotions of sadness and hopelessness would start to affect anybody they encounter. Such negative vibes could spread like wildfire, and eventually and in some cases, this would result in suicide or violence toward themselves or others. The same study reported that 31 percent of LGBT youth considered attempting suicide in the past year, as opposed to 14 percent of heterosexual youth.

The West Virginia University's School of Public Health and the state's Bureau for Public Health's Division of Tobacco Prevention reported this year that nearly 41 percent of people in the LGBT community smoked, as opposed to 23.9 percent of the state's general population. The study also included that reasons for such a high number of smokers in the LGBT community includes bullying and homophobia, which can drive people to smoke. From every indication, fear of not accepting people of different sexual orientation can contribute to our society's ill health.

From a theological standpoint, Luke 6:37 noted, "Judge not, and you shall not be judged. Condemn not, and you shall not be contemned. Forgive, and you will be forgiven." This means that we should not judge each other irrespective of our views and opinions. This message from the Bible existed in the New Testament, suggesting we should not impose our beliefs on others. Only God has the sovereignty to judge.

Evidently, when we judge others for whatever reasons, chances are, the judged would experience some emotions such as anger, rage, betrayal, and so forth. If those emotions are not addressed, it can have a spillover effect. In other words, the judged would transfer rage or anger to somebody else, oftentimes to people closer to him or her (for example, a partner, coworker, and so forth).

In 2009, Robert T. Muller, PhD, reported that Zukiswa Gaca, a twenty-year-old lesbian in South Africa, decided to take her own life by lying down on the local train tracks after she had been raped for the second time—a victim of corrective rape. Corrective rape is a criminal practice in South African culture, whereby men rape lesbian women—a criminal exercise to "cure" the woman of her sexual orientation. Such heinous crimes are committed around the world, including Ecuador, Russia, and many African countries. By implication, when we fail to identify others for who they are, we indirectly contribute to the violent behaviors of such people. Therefore, the fear of identifying the truth has consequences in our lives and the lives of others. It also perpetuates violent behaviors.

Is Violence a Learned Behavior?

We learn by doing and experiencing what we have heard or visualized. That's why children from abusive homes, for example, are more prone to perpetuating what they have observed while growing up. The same applies to relationships.

- A spouse who experiences violence in a relationship tends to live a defensive life in his or her next relationship, whereby preparing to defend himself or herself against his or her new spouse.

- An employee who works in a hostile environment tends to walk around the office tense.
- A victim of school bullying walks around anticipating the defense of himself or herself from being bullied.

The scenarios presented have potential of resulting in violent behaviors. We focus this section on addressing how we contribute to learned violent behaviors in social settings, workplaces, and schools. The *Journal of Abnormal and Social Psychology* shared an empirical study of social psychologists—Albert Bandura, PhD; Dorothea Ross, PhD; and Sheila Ross, PhD—on transmission of aggression through imitation of aggressive models. The result showed that children imitated the behavior of a model in the presence of the model.

When the study was repeated a few years later to see the degree of imitation when the model was not there, the evidence suggested that nursery school children exposed to aggressive behavior models tended to imitate not only their aggressiveness but other behaviors as well (Bandura et al. 1964). This is evidence that violent behaviors happening all over the United States supports researchers' empirical study that violence is a learned behavior. People who imitate others are called "copycats," which means people imitate behaviors, especially violent ones. How do we contribute to this behavior?

We contribute to violent behaviors when we ignore the very things that provoke such behaviors. For example, the

New England Journal of Medicine identified the Newtown school shooting as a combination of a withdrawn and isolated individual who was emotionally charged with anger and rage. In the case of Newtown, the individual who committed such a heinous crime had subtle symptoms (withdrawn and isolated) and other issues as experts identified. Experts found that information after investigation of the case.

The issue of gun violence in the media is another challenge. Experts are trying to educate the public to understand that early diagnoses of mental illnesses and social withdrawal and isolation could help minimize such tragedies as the Newtown shooting and other violent attacks around the globe. When we fail to listen to these voices of reason, we act on the inconvenient truth.

When we fear to push Washington (lawmakers) to pass gun control, such as bans or controls on assault weapons, we also act on the inconvenient truth. By implication, we directly or indirectly contribute to the perpetuation of violence in our country. These are real threats to human peace and emotional stability. How can we as a human race, irrespective of demographics (race, religion, gender, sexual orientation, and so forth), take charge and contribute to a broader cause of maintaining peace, starting from impacting people in our circle, neighborhoods, cities, states, countries, and the world? We can discuss possible recommendations to these issues using two practical psychological constructs: spirituality and emotional intelligence.

Spiritual Solutions to External Challenges

Spiritual engagements control life's journey. In other words, our internal space controls what happens in our external environments. And you have the most to do with what happens to you in life. Therefore, the issues discussed in this chapter are sensitive and thought provoking, but they can be solved by tapping into spiritual exercises and God's given unlimited life choices. A theological approach to these choices suggests that, as adults, we live by our own choices and not the decisions of others. Conversely, we live by the consequences of our choices. Theological evidence supports the notion of choices and consequences.

- Joshua 24:15 states, "And if it seems evil to you to serve the LORD, choose for yourselves this day whom you will serve, whether the gods which your fathers served that were on the other side of the River, or the gods of the Amorites, in whose land you dwell. But as for me and my house, we will serve the LORD."
- Leviticus 20:13 profoundly declares, "If a man lies with a male as he lies with a woman, both of them have committed an abomination. They shall surely be put to death. Their blood shall be upon them."
- John 8:7 states, "He who is without sin among you, let him throw a stone at her first."
- Matthew 7:1–5 notes, "Judge not, that you be not judged. For with what judgment you judge, you will

be judged; and with the measure you use, it will be measured back to you. And why do you look at the speck in your brother's eye, but do not consider the plank in your own eye? Or how can you say to your brother, let me remove the speck from your eye; and look, a plank is in your own eye? Hypocrite! First remove the plank from your own eye, and then you will see clearly to remove the speck from your brother's eye."

- Romans 6:1–2 notes, "What shall we say then? Shall we continue in sin that grace may abound? Certainly not!"
- Proverbs 14:12 reads, "There is a way that seems right to a man, But its end is the way of death."

These few verses point to the fact that, as we make our beds, so we must lie on them. There is a payday, and that day suggests that there is a God who knows the secrets of the heart (Ps. 44:21). And God gave us the spirit of discernment, which can be translated in a psychological term as emotional intelligence.

Emotional Intelligence

Daniel Goleman, PhD, author of *Emotional Intelligence: Why It Can Matter More Than IQ*, stated that emotional intelligence is more important than intelligence quotient (IQ). Emotional intelligence creates self-awareness, altruism, personal motivation, empathy, and so forth. Joseph Olusola Adesina, PhD, defined emotional intelligence as the ability to perceive, control, and evaluate emotions. In other words, emotions regulate our success in life. They can direct us to make mistakes in life, or they can lead us to make sound judgments, but it all depends on how emotionally intelligent we are. In terms of fear as one of our emotions, applying emotional intelligence to navigate through our fears, we can analyze, dissect, critique, and observe our fears to make decisions that could be less negative, more rewarding, and impactful.

When we run into difficult situations as the issues of LGBT and violence, we can approach them using emotional intelligence to observe how we feel about them and how others could possibly view them. Analyzing the issues from different scopes will allow us to make sound decisions and interact with others more peacefully and constructively without relying too much on social dogma and personal biases. Using spirituality and emotional intelligence to tackle issues of life such as the inconvenient truth would prepare us to view our challenges from a holistic lens.

In summary, we discussed our inactions to cultural shift such as the LGBT community's expressions for public acceptance and the way violence is a learned behavior. Those are the inconvenient truths because we feared to take a position when it came to controversial issues. In other words, when life presents certain issues to us, especially circumstances that contradict our beliefs, we tend to justify our actions based on memorized emotions, ones that suggest that new information requires extra energy and critical thinking. Interestingly, humans accept change only if such change is familiar and favorable. But when such change is unfamiliar and unorthodox, we resist it. Throughout this text, we used evidence-based studies to bring these issues to the limelight.

The intent of this chapter is not to sway your opinion. Rather, it is to challenge your way of thinking and open a new conversation and imagination on how we fear unfamiliar situations. It is considered unfamiliar because we have not considered the what-ifs? What if what we know is based on limited knowledge? What if we stop judging and start forgiving, what could happen to the old and new imagination? Now it is your turn to make a sound decision based on provided information in this chapter. Hopefully, the awareness and new imagination provided in this chapter can either strengthen your position or encourage you to consider new approaches to these issues. Whatever decision you made, you have adjusted to the new information as humans are constantly entertaining new information and adjusting to the changes life offer us. These changes are why Mother Nature offers us day and night, the four seasons of the year, and the dry and rainy seasons.

In other words, if Mother Nature permanently offers us one season, then we will stop learning. And when we stop learning, we stop producing at maximum capacity. And when we stop producing, we literally die. Progressively, we cannot use yesterday's victory to fight today's challenges.

Rather, we produce new ideas on a daily basis to solve issues that are facing us at that moment in time. For these reasons, we are constantly maladjusting.

The next chapter presents the need to be maladjusted, which means we are constantly adjusting to current situations because we are not satisfactorily adjusted to one particular environment and conditions of life. Refusing to adjust to particular environments and conditions of life is evidence that we are growing, as the following examples show:

- People move from state to state because they constantly adjust to changing situations.
- A single man decides to marry or settle down because he fears fixating on loneliness.
- A young woman decides to sign up for a college degree program because she sees better days ahead of her and not behind her.
- A person hunts for a job because he or she wants something new.
- Organizations merge because they fear going out of business.
- People make friends because they fear losing friends.

The list is endless. Maladjusted is a dance of life, a beat that we become stagnant and unproductive if we stop dancing. Therefore, let us embrace the idea of being maladjusted to situations of life.

Chapter 11

Maladjusted

Life is full of adjustments that make life exciting, challenging, engaging, frightening, fulfilling, and empowering. In this chapter, we will address the importance of embracing adjustments and identifying ways of making practical and strategic moves toward minimizing unnecessary and retrogressive adjustments. In other words, certain situations are unavoidable while some are calculative. Knowing the signs of constructive adjustments would help us minimize the risks associated with maladjusting. In order to simplify this topic of maladjustment, we will use life experiences to illustrate the significance of paying attention to conscious adjustments and understanding when destructive fear of adjustment can handicap a person.

Maladjustment in the context of a conventional approach is relative to how we live on a daily basis. When we are not satisfactorily adjusted, it pushes us to seek new information and new imagination. New information provides change to existing circumstance. Whenever we receive new information, we tend to respond differently as an indication of shift in thought process.

To practicalize the experience of maladjustment, we would discuss an immigrant man from East Africa seeking a greener pasture in the United States of America. His whole journey from East Africa to the States was full of adjustments. The one time he ignored the need for adjusting to new information and situations triggered a reaction from his loved ones. Maybe your case might not be from a loved one. Maybe it's a coworker, client, or complete stranger. The message of paying attention to your surroundings and responding or adjusting to new information is critical.

The Uncertainties of Maladjustments

Denzi migrated from East Africa into the United States of America on a visiting visa, seeking a better life. Denzi was raised in an economically deprived home. His parents had big dreams for Denzi to go to school and become a medical doctor, but his parents had no financial means of sending him to college. But fortunately, Denzi was a hardworking guy who owned a postcard, calling cards, and souvenir shop in front of the US embassy in his hometown. Due to his optimistic and cheerful views about life, he befriended embassy workers and several other people who visited the embassy while seeking traveling visas.

After ten years of selling souvenirs, postcards, and calling cards, he decided to ask the embassy workers what he would need to do to obtain a visiting visa to the States.

Fortunately for Denzi, he met their requirements, and they issued him a three-month visiting visa to the States. Upon arrival, he experienced cultural shock, loneliness, and language difficulties associated with living in a foreign land. He worked his way into the system and was favored by his friends.

Within twelve years of living in America, he assisted his parents financially and sent his siblings through college. As a vibrant man who loved education so much, he went back to school and graduated with a bachelor's degree in electrical engineering. His efforts paid off when he secured a job at an engineering company. Things were working out great for a thirty-eight-year-old Denzi. After two years of working for an engineering company with no wife or children, he decided to travel back to his homeland in search of a wife.

Denzi's visit to his homeland was memorable as he met Fatima, a beautiful woman who had recently graduated from a nursing program. Denzi immediately connected with her. They enjoyed each other's company and shared experiences about life and their academic journeys. Fatima, on the other hand, demonstrated the magic of a great cook and caring woman. Within weeks of Denzi's arrival, he added weight as a result of her cooking magic and caring demeanor. Vacation photos they took together were evidence of Denzi's memorable experience in his homeland.

As his three weeks of vacation was ending, Fatima's hospitable treatment mesmerized Denzi. Out of excitement and certainty, he expressed his interest to marry her.

Without hesitation, she agreed. Evidently, the United States of America is a land of opportunities and land of the free. Fatima had heard these words about America, and she was hysterical when Denzi proposed marriage. When he was getting ready to depart to the States, Fatima felt she was losing him into thin air, and she cried uncontrollably as his flight disappeared in a thick cloud of the night.

When Denzi arrived in the United States, he could not wait to call Fatima. Emotion of love was raging through his soul, and the question of "When will I see her again?" was racing through his mind. Denzi spent hours on the phone with Fatima, reminiscing and perambulating on the ecstasy of love. After a couple of visits to Fatima, they finally married and traveled together to America.

Denzi and Fatima were happily married. Their marriage was phenomenal and the envy of their community. As an engineer, Denzi was predictable, calculative, and disciplined. He was all about measurements and precision. Fatima as a nurse, on the other hand, was all about working overtime at work and making as much money as she possibly could. As expectations from friends and family might have it, Fatima conceived. It was the joyous moment of their lives. Denzi and Fatima went on a shopping spree the moment the doctor pronounced the pregnancy as a baby girl. Denzi was a bit unsure how to handle the added responsibility of his household, especially now that the baby was on the way. Their situation shifted when they had a baby daughter and Fatima was on maternity leave for twelve weeks.

Denzi and Fatima's marriage had an unexpected turn when they both lost interest in each other. Denzi complained that Fatima did not like to spend time with him ever since the baby was born. Fatima complained about Denzi's failure to understand her new situation with their new baby. Fatima accused Denzi of emotional aloofness and being critical about everything. Tension intensified, and Denzi felt like an outsider in his own house. Fatima felt like Denzi was having an extramarital affair. That was why he distanced himself from her and the baby.

What do you think happened between Denzi and Fatima? Were they incompatible? Did they fall out of love? Was money the issue? These are basic questions to ask when such situations arise. If you guess any of these questions could be right, you may be correct. But let's dive deeper into the matter of the issue.

If you noticed, all this while, Denzi and Fatima had been adjusting to situations as new information was presented. Denzi settled in America and established himself by legalizing his stay, graduating from college, securing a job, and financially stabilizing his siblings and parents. When he visited home to seek a wife, he achieved that and brought Fatima to America. Their problems started when they failed to adjust to the arrival of their new baby daughter.

Notice that their problems were not incompatibility; nor did they fall out of love. Instead, they stopped adjusting to the new information and situation, the arrival of their newborn. In other words, they failed to adjust to accommodate their daughter. Instead of asking the right questions, they started asking the wrong ones, whereby missing the root cause of their problem.

This is a primary example of what happens when we stop adjusting to new information. The moment we stop entertaining new information, we start living in the past with old information, thereby fixating our progress on old information and failing to maladjust.

Personalized Maladjustment

Can you recollect when you experienced similar situations when you stopped adjusting to conditions of life? For example, you confront your spouse for not loving you the way he or she used to. If you pay attention to your concern, you will realize that something major must have happened and you failed to adjust to the current situation. Or you set your expectations too high to the extent of becoming unrealistic.

Imagine when you first married your spouse fifteen years ago. You two used to hike twelve miles every weekend, for example, but now you could hardly hike five miles. Evidently, several factors have played a role, such as age, children rearing, and different levels of stress. These three stressors can be unavoidably expected. But failure to realistically acknowledge the obvious and refusal to adjust to the new information could create challenges and dogmatic experience.

Consider this example. You bought a trampoline for your children, and they played on it—day in and day out—for three years. You noticed the trampoline was sagging as a result of your children constantly jumping on it for three years. Will you discipline your children for the sagging trampoline, or will you either replace or adjust the trampoline? The same principle applies in our lives. When we fail to adjust to changing conditions, we tend to shift blame on somebody or something else.

There is an urgent need for us to be cognizant of changing conditions in life. In other words, maladjustment is necessary. It is the *sin qua non* of life (something you cannot do without). We should not fear to adjust to circumstances of life because life constantly changes.

According to a research study reported in the *Journal of Family Psychology* (2012), there is an association between relationship adjustment and life satisfaction. The study noted that life satisfaction also plays a role in relationship adjustment. This means that, whenever a couple finds themselves not adjusting to situations of life, such inability to adjust will affect life satisfaction. In other words, if you are not satisfied and not adjusting to changing conditions, you will likely struggle in relationship adjustment. Therefore, relationship adjustment is linked to life satisfaction, and it predicts a happier marital adjustment.

It is highly advisable to read the work of researchers Scott M. Stanley, Erica P. Ragan, Galena K. Rhoades, and Howard J. Markman in the *Journal of Family Psychology* (2012). It has an in-depth knowledge of life satisfaction and relationship adjustment points. Due to the extensive nature of their research study, it is advisable to read it at your leisure.

The quest to maladjust is a great element of success. In other words, being flexible to change in a relationship, workplace, or social setting has a rewarding effect and brings some level of satisfaction in life.

- In the workplace, employees willing to volunteer to help others are likely the first to be considered for promotion when opportunity presents itself.
- In social settings, friends making themselves available to assist are likely the ones their friends will depend on when situation arises.

So don't be afraid of adjusting to conditions of life because, if you refuse to adapt, change will still occur anyway. In Denzi and Fatima's situation, because of their refusal to accommodate their newborn baby, they changed from being happily married to finding fault in their relationship. So either way, change will take place, whether positive or negative.

This chapter was intended to create awareness on how minor adjustments to life can bring a significant change in the way we view maladjustment. Fear of adjusting to situations depends on what direction change is directed. In other words, are you being constructively afraid, or are you being destructively afraid to adjust? But in any situation, change is constant.

From historical perspectives, great men were not afraid of adjusting to changing conditions. Maladjusting to life circumstance is a sign of greatness. Even Jesus Christ feared. There are accounts in the Bible when he feared. Especially when he was on his way to be crucified, he still overcame his obstacles by adjusting to changing conditions of life—for example, by accepting the task that his heavenly Father sent him to earth to perform. From biblical accounts, he was sent to die for our sins so we may live life more abundantly (John 10:10, 1 Pet. 2:24, Rom. 4:25, Col. 1:22, and so forth). He went through several adjustments before accomplishing his mission. Therefore, maladjustments of life are inevitable, and the approach to which we choose to adjust justifies the result.

The next chapter discusses fear from a perspective of relevance as it relates to Jesus in human flesh. It explains how fear is no respecter of persons because Jesus feared. The intent of this chapter is to draw attention to the fact that, if Jesus feared, nobody could claim a fearless life.

Therefore, as we read this chapter, consider yourself lucky if you do have a strong emotion called fear. The challenge to that effect is what you fear and how you embrace it—either from a pessimistic or optimistic approach. If you can identify your fears early enough in any situation, chances are, you can make a healthier decision relating to sound judgment and healthier living.

Chapter 12

Jesus Feared

I interviewed several pastors from various denominations to ensure that this chapter is consistent with the topic/content empirically discussed. Biblical references were primarily the source of discussion. And to stay within the context of this book, it was necessary to keep this chapter focused and short. The objective is to draw particular attention to the inescapable hold of fear in our lives and how Jesus, while in human flesh, feared and adjusted to the conditions required to achieve his goal. His adjustment to the conditions of life depicts the importance of constructive fear.

Jesus adjusted to the conditions of life when he was on earth in human flesh. He came down to earth as human flesh so he may relate with us. When he interacted with the oppressed, he related with them on a human level and was able to meet them at their point of needs. In other words, he never portrayed himself as more superior. Rather, he humbled himself. When Mary and Martha called him to resurrect their brother Lazarus from death, he came on the scene as human and wept over Lazarus's death. He consoled Mary and Martha before calling Lazarus to come forth (John 11:1–45). Although he knew he had the power to resurrect Lazarus from the dead, he still demonstrated to Mary, Martha, and believers that he could still relate to their pains and struggles. Therefore, he was constantly changing to the conditions of life to meet believers at the point of their needs.

I principally wrote this chapter to demonstrate that it is human to fear. In other words, as long as we are in this world and interacting with the elements of this world, we will always experience fear, whether constructive or destructive. Theologically, Jesus feared when he was human flesh. It was on that account that this chapter is written.

From a philosophical standpoint, we can relate to Jesus's journey while he was on earth as our experience. When he was chastised and humiliated on his way to the cross, he experienced fear of abandonment from his heavenly Father. In Matthew 26:39, Jesus was in such excruciating pain that he prayed to his heavenly Father. "O my father, if it is possible, let this cup pass from me; nevertheless, not as will but as you will." In Matthew 27:46, about the ninth hour while on the cross, he pleaded to his heavenly Father, *"Eli, Eli, lama sabachtani* (My God, My God, why have you forsaken me)?" Biblical references support the claim that Jesus feared. Other relevant experiences and research studies make a strong case to show how fear can lead to greatness if managed well.

Fear Management

A peer-reviewed research study suggested that the key factor in fear management is controllability (Goud 2005). This means that, when we feel we are in control of our situations, we tend to manage our fear constructively. In other words, fear can only be destructive when we feel we are not in control of the situation. For example, we fail exams when we feel lack of control on the topics to read about, inability to rest before sitting for a test, ill preparation beforehand, and so forth. Therefore, if we want to manage our fears, we must first manage the circumstances that lead to the event.

Although some situations are unpredictable and unavoidable, the Goud (2005) study emphasized that developing confidence and self-efficacy and having a sense of purpose are potent forces for counteracting fears. Therefore, it is critical that we understand the role of confidence and controllability when it comes to fear management. When a life situation seems difficult and unsure, the best approach to managing such a situation is to generate a mind-set that this situation cannot be the end of the world. Rather, it is a temporary situation. It can also be referred to as systematic desensitization, understanding that difficult situations are part of human DNA and cannot be completely avoided.

From a theological standpoint, the intent of this chapter is not to discredit Jesus's work on earth. Rather, it is to draw comparison as to why fear is inevitable in our lives and why it has such a strong hold that it needs to be redirected to work to our benefit. When Jesus feared, he was able to redirect his fear to his heavenly Father by reminding himself why he was suffering in the first place. The moment he engaged and aligned himself with his goal, he allowed fear to take him to his aim, dying for our sins (Rom. 4:25).

Therefore, if he did not complete his Calvary experience, it would be an aborted experience. In this context, Jesus feared not to abort his earthly mission by sticking with his painful experience so we may have life and more abundantly. 1 Peter 3:18 notes, "For Christ also suffered once for sins, the just for the unjust, that he might bring us to God, being put to death in the flesh but made alive by the spirit." Jesus's cross experience depicted him in human form for our sake, and in the midst of his pains, he had the human experience of fear and suffering.

In the context of Jesus's fearful episodes, his response to his fear made his fear constructive. In other words, when he was in human flesh, he observed his fear by acknowledging and admitting his painful experiences, yet he understood that he had control over fear and fear did not have control over him. His control over fear compelled him to use affirmative words such as "Father not my will, but your will be done" and "Father let this cup pass over me." These affirmations prepared him to finish his pains and fears with hope and certainty.

Think of situations when fear enveloped your mind and you reacted pessimistically. In the end, the very thing you feared happened. On the other hand, recollect a difficult event where you showed some level of optimism. Because of your optimistic approach to that event, you overcame the obstacle. This is evidence that we have control over our fears. Fear is nothing except a state of the mind because it is possible that we see our circumstances the way we are and not the way the circumstances are. For example, when preparing for an exam, we are already engulfing ourselves with fear of failing, especially if we have ill feelings about those subjects. Therefore, we fail to see the exams for what they are. Instead, we tend to associate our inadequacies with those subjects.

In other words, rather than saying "I am sitting for a challenging test," we are known to say, "I fear math, statistics, and calculus; therefore, I will never be good at it." We have just professed failure into our situation. Because of negative confession, we will be ill prepared for the exams and, sure enough, flunk the tests. But when we approach the challenge for what it is without associating our entire existence to that very problem, we are bound to engage in exercises that would position us to overcome such fear. One of the ways to overcome such fear is to devote more time to studying for the subjects or hiring a math tutor. When we do these things, we would realize that, the more exposure we give to our difficult situations, the better and less fearful we become to them.

Based on what you have read so far, I challenge you to rethink how you view fear. If you view fear from constructive perspective (as an inevitable ingredient in our tasteful delicacy), we will triumph over fear each time we experience difficult moments. Thomas Edison entertained fear on several occasions until he overcame it after 999 times of trying. Today, we enjoy his ingenuity of electricity because he feared that, if he settled to fail, then electricity would be a thing of illusion. Instead, he refused to allow fear to rob the world of electricity.

What is your biggest fear in life? Are you feeding your fears with negativisms and self-doubts, or are you entertaining them with new imagination and crafty optimism? Overcoming our fears opens doors for millions of others to follow, those who thought winning was only for the wealthy and opportune. But if we do what others did and succeed, we can succeed as well. At the same time, by allowing our fears to defeat us, we shut doors to millions of people. Therefore, the world will be a better place if we allow our light to shine without minding how many times we failed. After all, we are remembered by what we do exceptionally well, whether a destructive or constructive act. I would rather be remembered for contributing to the body of knowledge than robbing from history the great achievements others have contributed.

Going back to the title of this chapter, if Jesus would have given up faith and hope on his way to Calvary (while as human flesh), his name would not be remembered in Christendom as Messiah. Rather, he would have been remembered as a mere story in the Bible. Such stories in the Bible omitted the names of the players and replaced their names with statements like these:

- "A certain man lame from his mother's womb was carried, whom they laid daily at the gate of temple which is called beautiful, to ask for alms from those who entered the temple" (Acts 3:2).
- "Now a certain woman had a flow of blood for twelve years" (Mark 5:25).
- "Now a woman, having a flow of blood for twelve years, who had spent all her livelihood on physicians and could not be healed by any" (Luke 8:43).

Notice that their names were omitted because of their insignificance. Instead, scholars encouraged Bible readers and believers to print their own names where those men and women's names would have been written and claim the same blessings they had.

I challenge you to make a name for yourself. The world will remember you forever, and the only way to contribute to the body of knowledge is to entertain fear to work for you rather than work against you. Whenever you run into problems, ask yourself, *Am I responding to this situation constructively or destructively?* If you monitor your response to fears, it will become a habit over time to face fearful conditions from a constructive rather than destructive perspective.

As we conclude this chapter, it marks the last chapter of this book. On the next page, we share final thoughts as we have read twelve strategies on how to view fear from different perspectives. It also marks the beginning of a new imagination.

Closing Thoughts

I put together this piece of work in the hope that readers would gain fresh ideas on how to view fear from constructive perspectives. In other words, not all fears are negative or destructive. Oftentimes, we run into emotional paralysis when we react to an event based on memorized emotions, especially when such an event is negative and uncertain. These emotions are evidence of events that we either encountered or witnessed others experience. Therefore, we personalized them to be our stories. Unfortunately, when we act on the premise of distorted views, we tend to miscalculate or overly inflate an event. And when an event or experience is exaggerated, anxiety, tension, and fear become inevitable.

By reading this book, you should have a general idea that fear can be managed, especially when you feel you are in control of the situation. Destructive fear creeps in when we are unable to pull cognitive scripts for whatever experience we are going through. In other words, we panic when we do not have any point of reference to whatever situation that life presents to us.

This book should also teach you to look for positive outcomes in uncertain and unpredictable situations. Anecdotes and evidence-based studies shared in this text were intended to suggest that constructive fear produces confidence, optimism, insightful and encouraging results as opposed to destructive fear, which increases anxiety, pessimism, low self-esteem, and a whole host of other negative emotions.

Great men and women mentioned in this book should be sources of hope and inspiration, suggesting we are not the only people who are going through life challenges. Others have gone through similar (if not worse) situations and survived them. Because of their bravery, the world is learning from their experiences, and these experiences are made available to you in book form.

I wrote this book in simple terms so readers could enjoy it and share it with friends, family members, colleagues, cohorts, peers, and anybody who has interest in learning. I wrote this book out of a sincere desire to assist others. It will be a great delight to know that the book has contributed to improving the quality of life of anybody who yearns for a change and a new beginning. I am convinced that, if the principles and shared knowledge demonstrated in this book are applied, chances are, positive change would prevail.

We may never meet in person, but my work has virtually brought us together. May the time you spend reading this book add value to your life and the lives of others you meet.

References

Preface

ClinicQuotes. "Forced Abortion 3: Violence Can Lead to Murder." http://clinicquotes.com/forced-abortion-3-violence-can-lead-to-murder.

Markway, B. 2012. "Getting over Stage Fright: Becoming an Effective Public Speaker." *Psychology Today.* http://www.psychologytoday.com/blog/shyness-is-nice/201202/getting-over-stage-fright-becoming-effective-public-speaker.

PublicSpeakingSkills. 2013. "Public Speaking: The Number 1 Fear—Part 1." http://www.publicspeakingskills.com/pages/articles/public%20speaking%20-%20the%20number%201%20fear%20-%20part%20i.htm.

Chapter 1

Firestein, S. 2012. *Ignorance: How It Drives Science.* New York: Oxford University Press.

Richard, D. 2007. "Don't Be Afraid to Look Fear in the Face." *Daily Telegraph*, August 30. http://www.

telegraph.co.uk/finance/markets/2953206/Dont-be-afraid-to-look-fear-in-the-face.html.

Bobinski, D. 2003. "Management-Issues: A Cure for Micromanagement." http://www.management-issues. com/opinion/691/a-cure-for-micro-management/.

Chapter 2

Cestnick, T. 2003. "Break the Poverty Mentality for a Good Cause." *The Globe and Mail*, November 22. http:// www.theglobeandmail.com/globe-investor/investment-ideas/break-the-poverty-mentality-for-a-good-cause/ article774021/.

Dvorsky, G. 2007. "Sentient Developments: Managing Your 50,000 Daily Thoughts." Accessed March 9, 2013. http://www.sentientdevelopments.com/2007/03/ managing-your-50000-daily-thoughts.html.

Trevor, T. M., Jerry Cha-Jan Change, and Deborah K. Smith. 2006. "Clarifying the Role of Self-Efficacy and Metacognition as Predictors of Performance: Construct Development and Test." *Database for Advances in Information Systems* 37 (2): 125–32. http://search. proquest.com/docview/196635578?accountid=35812.

Kunst, J. 2012. "Is Your Glass Half Empty or Half Full? How Therapy Helps Us Change Perspective." Accessed January 2, 2013. http://www.psychologytoday. com/blog/headshrinkers-guide-the-galaxy/201203/ is-your-glass-half-empty-or-half-full.

WiseGeek. 2003. "Clear Answers for Common Questions: What Is Poverty Mentality?" Accessed January 2, 2013. http://www.wisegeek.org/what-is-poverty-mentality.htm.

Chapter 3

Farino, K. 2012. *Thank God for Another Day: The Miracle Breakthrough*. Mustang, OK: Tate Publishing.

Copeda, M. 2012. "Shine: 7 Divorce Myths—Debunked!" http://shine.yahoo.com/love-sex/7-divorce-myths-8212-debunked-170300654.html.

Chapter 4

Firestein, S. 2012. *Ignorance: How It Drives Science*. New York: Oxford University Press.

Vujicic, N. 2013. "Life without Limbs: From No Limbs to No Limit." http://www.lifewithoutlimbs.org/about-nick.

HarvestTV. 2008. "Greg Laurie and Nick Vujicic: Life without Limbs." http://www.youtube.com/watch?v=a8 Cwx2UbTJA&feature=youtu.be.

Vickers, A. 2011. *People vs. the State of Illusion*. Exalt Films.

Parker, John. 2011. "The 9 Billion-People Question." *The Economist*, February 24. http://www.economist.com/node/18200618.

Chapter 5

The Library of Congress. 2010. "Family Tragedy." http://www.loc.gov/exhibits/americancolony/amcolony-family.html.

Vickers, A. 2011. *People vs. the State of Illusion*. Exalt Films.

Steinber, G., and L. Gano-Overway. 2003. "Developing Optimism Skills to Help Youths Overcome Adversity." *Journal of Physical Education, Recreation & Dance* 74 (5): 40–44. http://search.proquest.com/docview/215767 590?accountid=35812.

Chapter 6

Vickers, A. 2011. *People vs. the State of Illusion*. Exalt Films.

Stone, M. 2002. "Forgiveness in the Workplace." *Industrial and Commercial Training* 34 (6): 278–86. http://search.proquest.com/docview/214110348?accountid=35812.

Schruggs, C., and J. Scruggs. 2012. *I Do Again: How We Found a Second Chance at Our Marriage—and You Can Too*. Colorado Springs: Water Brook Press, 2012.

Shapiro, B. 2011. "Let Go of the Past: The Benefits of Forgiveness." *Washington Jewish Week* 47 (38): 37. http://search.proquest.com/docview/903304314?accountid=35812.

Philpot, C. 2006. "Intergroup Apologies and Forgiveness." Unpublished PhD thesis, Office of International Affairs America Psychological Association. http://www.apa.org/international/resources/forgiveness.pdf.

Chapter 7

Burkley, M. 2009. "Social Thinker: Why Don't We Help? Less Is More, At Least When It Comes to Bystanders." http://www.psychologytoday.com/blog/the-social-thinker/200911/why-don-t-we-help-less-is-more-least-when-it-comes-bystanders.

Jaffe, E. 2013. "Why Wait? The Science Behind Procrastination." *Association for Psychological Science Observer* 26 (4). http://www.psychologicalscience.org/index.php/publications/observer/2013/april-13/why-wait-the-science-behind-procrastination.html.

Chapter 8

McCallum, D. 2008. "Dealing with Healthy and Unhealthy Fears." *Kamloops Daily News*, November 29. http://search.proquest.com/docview/358617777?accountid=35812.

Goldsmith, B. 2008. "Dealing with Fear in the Workplace." *Cost Engineering* 50 (12): 21–22. http://search.proquest.com/docview/220461092?accountid=35812.

Duckworth, A. L., and L. Ekreis-Winkler. 2013. "True Grit." *Association for Psychological Science Observer* 26 (4). http://www.psychologicalscience.org/index.php/publications/observer/2013/april-13/true-grit.html.

American Psychological Association. 2013. *Facing the School Dropout Dilemma*. http://apa.org/pi/families/resources/school-dropout-prevention.aspx?item=1.

Lowe, D. R. 2010. A qualitative ethnographic study of african american male high school dropouts. University of Phoenix). ProQuest Dissertations and Theses, , 182. Retrieved from http://search.proquest.com/docview/853641949?accountid=35812. (853641949).

Chapter 9

Southwick, S. M., and D. S. Charney. 2012. "Resilience. The Science of Mastering Life's Greatest Challenges." *Facing Fear: An Adaptive Response*. Cambridge: Cambridge University Press.

Akpan-Obong, P. 2013. *Letters to Nigeria: Journal of an African Woman in America*. North Charleston, SC: Create Space.

Morisano, D., J. B. Hirsh, J. B. Peterson, R. O. Pihl, and B. M. Shore. 2010. "Setting, Elaborating, and Reflecting on Personal Goals Improves Academic Performance." *Journal of Applied Psychology* 95 (2): 255–64. doi: http://dx.doi.org/10.1037/a0018478.

Choman, A. 2007. "Renowned Poet Maya Angelou Captivates Audience." *Citizens' Voice*, November 3.

http://search.proquest.com/docview/356785418?accou ntid=35812.

Eaton, C. 1994. "Poet Angelou Shares Her Roots in Hub Visit." *Bay State Banner*, March 3. http://search. proquest.com/docview/367259859?accountid=35812.

Belser, A. 2012. "Boomers Average 11.3 Jobs in a Lifetime, Study Finds." *McClatchy-Tribune Business News*, July 26. http://search.proquest.com/docview/1027859664?ac countid=35812.

Lucariello, J. 2013. "How Do My Students Think: Diagnosing Student Thinking." American Psychological Association. http://www.apa.org/education/k12/ student-thinking.aspx?item=13.

Chapter 10

Almeida, J., R. M. Johnson, H. L. Corliss, B. E. Molnar, and D. Azrael. 2009. "Emotional Distress among LGBT Youth: The Influence of Perceived Discrimination Based on Sexual Orientation." *Journal of Youth and Adolescence* 38 (7): 1001–14. http://search.proquest. com/docview/204636129?accountid=35812.

Buffie, W. C. 2011. "Public Health Implications of Same-Sex Marriage." *American Journal of Public Health* 101 (6): 986–90. http://search.proquest.com/docview/86782 5961?accountid=35812.

Kersey, L. 2013. "Report: State's LGBT Smoking Rate Higher than General Population." *McClatchy—Tribune*

Business News, February 15. http://search.proquest. com/docview/1287977735?accountid=35812.

Bandura, A., D. Ross, and S. A. Ross. 1961. "Transmission of Aggression through Imitation of Aggressive Models." *The Journal of Abnormal and Social Psychology* 63 (3): 575–82. doi: http://dx.doi.org/10.1037/h0045925.

Muller, R. 2013. "Fixing Gay: 'Corrective Rape' in South Africa." *Psychology Today: Talking About Trauma. The causes, treatment, prevention, and implications of trauma.* Accessed October 5, 2013. http://www.psychologytoday. com/blog/talking-about-trauma/201305/ fixing-gay-corrective-rape-in-south-africa.

Walkup, J. T., and D. H. Rubin. 2013. "Social Withdrawal and Violence—Newtown, Connecticut." *The New England Journal of Medicine* 368 (5): 399–401. http:// search.proquest.com/docview/1312500942?accoun tid=35812.

Adesina, O. J. 2012. "Emotional Intelligence, Locus of Control and Conflict Handling Skills as Predictors of Non-violent Behaviour among University Students in South-western Nigeria." *Ife Psychologia* 20 (2): 31–38.

Goleman, D. 1995. *Emotional Intelligence: Why It Can Matter More Than IQ*. New York: Random House.

Chapter 11

Stanley, S. M., E. P. Ragan, G. K. Rhoades, and H. J. Markman. 2012. "Examining Changes in Relationship

Adjustment and Life Satisfaction in Marriage." *Journal of Family Psychology* 26 (1): 165–70. doi: http://dx.doi.org/10.1037/a0026759.

Chapter 12

Goud, N. H. 2005. "Courage: Its Nature and Development." *Journal of Humanistic Counseling, Education and Development* 44 (1): 102–16. http://search.proquest.com/docview/212471512?accountid=35812.

About the Author

J. Ibeh Agbanyim, the founder of Focused Vision Consulting, LLC, has been a senior logistics associate at UPS for the past sixteen years. He is also a scholarly contributor and member of the review board for *Journal of Instructional Research* at Grand Canyon University, a member of University of Phoenix Mentor Program, and the author of *The Power of Engagement: How to Find Balance in Work and Life.* His book was featured in several media including *Phoenix Focus, The Write Up! #1 Urban Newspaper,* and *Saturday Punch,* a nationally circulated newspaper based in Lagos, Nigeria. Agbanyim is a distinguished award recipient from the Department of Psychology for his exemplary leadership and significant contribution to academic excellence at the University of Ibadan, the premier university in Nigeria. His work was presented at America Society for Quality (ASQ).

Agbanyim holds a master's degree in general psychology with emphasis in industrial and organizational (I-O) psychology. He is currently a PhD student in I-O psychology and a graduate affiliate of American Psychological Association, the Society for Industrial and Organizational Psychology, American Society for Training and Development, and many others. Agbanyim resides in Mesa, Arizona.

Index

M

N

O

P

Q

S